MW01484386

A Most Uninitiated Hillbilly

A Most Uninitiated Hillbilly

Wallen Bean

authorHOUSE®

AuthorHouse™
1663 Liberty Drive
Bloomington, IN 47403
www.authorhouse.com
Phone: 1-800-839-8640

© *2009 Wallen Bean. All rights reserved.*

No part of this book may be reproduced, stored in a retrieval system, or transmitted by any means without the written permission of the author.

First published by AuthorHouse   11/20/2009

ISBN: 978-1-4490-4960-7 (e)
ISBN: 978-1-4490-4959-1 (sc)
ISBN: 978-1-4490-4958-4 (hc)

Printed in the United States of America
Bloomington, Indiana

This book is printed on acid-free paper.

"*When you reach an advanced age and look back over your lifetime it can seem to have had a consistent order and plan, as though composed by some novelist. Events that when they occurred seemed accidental and of little importance turn out to be indispensable factors in the composition of a consistent plot. So who composed the plot?*

Schopenhauer suggests that just as your dreams are composed by an aspect of yourself of which your consciousness is unaware, so too your whole life is composed of the will within you. And just as people whom you will have met by chance became leading agents in the structuring of your life, so, too, will you have served unknowingly as an agent, giving meaning to the lives of others. The whole thing gears together like a big symphony, with everything structuring everything else. And Schopenhauer concludes that everything links to everything else, moved by the one will to life."

Joseph Campbell

Dedicated to my three musical sons, Charles, James and John who keep me singing, and to my wife, Christine, without whose help I could not have written this book.

Acknowledgments

I want to express my gratitude to my editor, Marsha McCabe, for the many hours she spent listening to and refining my stories, and to her husband, Robert, for his expertise in getting the book published. My thanks go to my cousins, June Crowder and Preston Bean, for pictures and information about early family history. Many friends have encouraged me through my writing process and, though I cannot name them all, I thank them deeply.

Introduction

Those who ministered beside Wallen Bean at the Inter-Church Council of Greater New Bedford for many years often pondered the source of his empathy for young people and his out-of-the-box creative solutions for everyday human problems. Wonder no more! Now a straightforward, tender and humorous book tells all. In his brief memoir "A Most Uninitiated Hillbilly", Wallen paints a picture of the colorful threads that made up the warp and woof of his well-rounded ministry. The first strand is his upbringing in West Virginia where he learned a wide variety of farming and carpentry skills, attended twelve grades of school, and felt a call to the Methodist ministry. The introspective passages about his youth are reminiscent of the bittersweet story of Jody Baxter's growing up told by Marjorie Kinnan Rawlings in The Yearling.

A second strand describing parsonage life rings true to other books by Massachusetts Methodists. Life in a West Roxbury parsonage for Wallen and Christine is very like life in the Dorchester parsonage Grace Nies Fletcher tells about in Preacher's Kids, and In My Father's House. And son Charlie struggling as a 'P.K.' in New Bedford would have felt a strong kinship to Fletcher's brother Ike Nies coping with his father's ministry. Wallen's Cape Cod fishing anecdotes reflect a minister's love for God's outdoors. Janet Gillespie in Make a Joyful Noise tells a similarly warm story—how Pop (Reverend Russell Wicks), a Methodist minister of a large church in Holyoke, piles his wife and at least five children into the "Artful Dodger", the family Dodge, and drives each summer to the enchanting old fishing village of Westport Point on the New England coast. The difference, of course, is that these other stories are told by the children. In "Hillbilly" the father—the minister himself—shares his point-of-view with us.

Through the third strand the reader discovers one of the key tools of Wallen's effective ministry—his strong belief in the power of small groups, discovered first as a youngster experiencing cooperation within his family. He illustrates how this belief served him well as a senior counselor at a Great Society Job Corps, as an industrial counselor helping with quality circles, and as pastor of a Quaker meeting. Wallen was part of a large body of religious leaders in the sixties and seventies in whom the concept of small groups rose like a ground swell. Robert Raines, director for many years of the Kirkridge Retreat and Study Center, was the best-known proponent of this ministerial style expressed in his 1961 volume New Life in the Church. Wallen's experiences in retreat ministry included surviving class 3 Hurricane Carol's 93 miles per hour winds at Methodist Rolling Ridge Retreat Center, Andover, Massachusetts with 125 teens in 1954.

The very readable memoir reveals that another key tool in this Massachusetts minister's tool belt is the West Virginia boyhood with its visionary attitudes towards stick-to-it-tiveness, problem-solving and courage still living deep in Wallen's heart. Credit for his love for people must also be paid in part to his education in the mountain schoolhouse. For no doubt there he was taught Leigh Hunt's immortal poem "Abou Ben Adhem" in which Abou expresses a philosophy Wallen has made his own—"But cheerily still; …'I pray thee, then, Write me as one who loves his fellow men.'"

—Pamela J. Cole

As a United Church of Christ minister in the Greater New Bedford area, Pamela Cole has known Wallen Bean since he came to the Inter-Church Council in 1972. At present she serves as the Interim Minister at Smith Neck Friends Meeting in Dartmouth, Massachusetts where Wallen and Christine Bean are members.

Chapter 1

The Land

I was born in Moorefield, West Virginia, a sheltered, isolated community of 1500 people living their lives in a deep river valley, a beautiful, languid place that lives inside me still. I was born at home, in the middle of a hard, cold winter on February 12, 1922, and hadn't a clue that I lived in the Appalachians and would one day be called a hick by the world outside. When I was two weeks old, my parents drove to my grandmother's house ten miles away so she could get a look at me. Though I was well covered in blankets, my feet were actually frostbitten when we arrived. That's how cold it gets there in the winter.

Moorefield may have been lonely but it is vivid and abundant with memory. The landscape, the seasons, the way my family was—these images are deep inside me and never leave. Moorefield sits on the South Branch Valley of the Potomac River and its hillsides are dotted with subsistence farms averaging 12 acres in size. The valley and hills and farms are framed by steep mountains covered with forests.

Look at a map and you'll see that little dot, Moorefield, about 60 miles south of Cumberland, Maryland, 60 miles west of Winchester, Virginia and 70 miles north of Harrisonburg. Those bigger cities simply serve to locate us; most people have never heard of us. The truth is, you cannot tell from a map what a gem of a town that little dot is.

The Potomac River drains north and makes a strange geological twist as it flows through the valley. One day, thousands of years ago, it decided not to cut across the mountains but, rather, it pushed through them.

The passage turned into a narrow trough-like gap many miles long and, naturally, we call it "The Trough."

The Trough actually begins ten miles below Moorefield and ends at Romney, West Virginia on the old East-West U.S. highway, Route 50. The river is usually calm but once in a while these calm waters surge from the low banks and spread over the valley. Long after I left home, Moorefield nearly drowned in the Great Flood of 1985. On this terrible day, water filled the valley from ridge to ridge and took with it some 10,000 head of livestock. They never had a chance, nor did the seven people who drowned trying to rescue others.

The gorge is several hundred feet deep and the South Branch flows in a narrow channel at the bottom. Steep walls of rock rise on either side, and on one sits a corridor with just enough land to support the towns of Moorefield, Franklin and Petersburg. The deep rich loam that washed down from the mountainsides feeds this fertile valley and keeps the lumber companies and farmers in business. Farms produced corn as tall as the corn in Iowa and cattle were fattened on rich clover. The railroad kept up a brisk pace, moving farm and forest products out—cattle, chickens and lumber—and bringing in feed and special lumber from the tropics needed by a local veneer plant. In my day Moorefield was chickens; today its chief industry is cabinet making.

As a local boy, I know a few things about chickens, especially as Moorefield became a major center for raising them. The mountain farms feed the packing plants with as many as 125,000 chickens a day. The buildings that house them by the thousands have automated feeding and watering systems. If the light is on, a chicken will eat 24 hours a day. The cry of a hawk will so panic the chickens, it can cause them to pile up in a corner by the hundreds and smother to death. Hence, music is piped in to cover the sound of the old hawks passing overhead.

A new highway now serves and connects the valley towns, our neighbors. At the upper end of the valley is Petersburg with its 1200 people. I can tell you about Petersburg in one sentence: It does not have enough registered Democrats to hold a caucus. Moorefield, on the other hand, does not have enough Republicans to hold a caucus. What we have in common, however, is our magnificent river valley.

The temperature of the river changes as it runs through the towns and the fish hang out where the water temperatures are best for them. Trout need water below 70 degrees and since Petersburg is closer to the mountains and cooler, they have an abundance of trout. As the water warms up below Petersburg, the small mouth bass thrive and dominate. The river originates on the West Virginia line south of Franklin, a pristine mountain village unchanged by modern development. This is the home of James O'Brien, author of "At Home in the Heart of Appalachia."

Caves are numerous on the eastern slope of the mountains, which is undermined by limestone, the most spectacular being the Seneca Caverns above Petersburg. Drilling for natural gas has resulted in pockets that are now used to store gas to maintain flow at peak hours. My son, Charles, who owns the family farm, receives $24 a year for storage.

Our corridor of land, fortunately, is not polluted by coal mining, but that is not the story in the rest of the state. Outsiders own most of West Virginia; residents own only one percent of the land. The face of the state, the one we show to visitors and residents, is pockmarked and scarred beyond recognition, a great, ugly blemish, due to strip mining.

The mining companies use machinery so large they actually move the top of the mountains to get at the seams. Although the companies are now required to restore the landscape, much of the earth is riddled with coal fragments, causing acid to leach and poison the streams. This prevents natural growth, and much of the state will be sterile for the indefinite future if we are not more careful. This is the place where I was born, warts and all. This is the place I will write about.

My Family

Orvon Ray Bean, my father, was born and grew up in nearby Fabius, on top of the mountain, and could see the view for 40 miles in every direction. Mostly he could see more trees. He finished eight grades in a one-room mountain school, then took six months of training to become a teacher. He accepted a position in the normal school in nearby Needmore on the other side of Simon Bean Mountain, teaching for five years in a one-room schoolhouse.

The school was in my mother's hometown, so as a kid she attended with great enthusiasm. It turns out Essye Reed fell in love with her teacher. She dropped out of school in the seventh grade to become a mother to her nine brothers and sisters and do domestic chores. Her own mother was not good at nurturing and running a household. (Needmore, by the way, is several miles down the mountain from where her teacher, Orvon, grew up, and she continued to see him.)

Essye's father, Benjamin, was the miller in Needmore and a prosperous man. He owned a country store as well as six farms, and had the best team of horses in town. The family was well taken care of by her father's various enterprises. Unfortunately, I never knew my maternal grandfather as he died at 56 of measles and pneumonia. Her father may have contracted malaria when he was in the army in Texas and it lay dormant. My uncle put him on quinine. When he got cold, his false teeth actually rattled.

My uncle Lee Heltzel became executor of his estate and was said to be a poor manager. Also, a family story has it that before his demise Grandfather Reed got into a quarrel with a man who threatened to sue. He must have been terrified because he signed over property deeds to the man's brother. Anyway, two years after his death, my grandmother was without money, and my parents took care of her for the rest of her life.

Medora had long dark hair she wore in a bun that reached her knees when she combed it out. As a child, I would be called upon to comb out the tangles. She chewed snuff and was warm and affectionate. Over the years, she took turns visiting her children but always returned to my home in Moorefield and called it her home. She is buried in the family cemetery in Baker's Run.

My father's family was dirt poor so I don't know how the romance between my father and mother went over with her wealthy father. My father's parents were subsistence mountain farmers. My grandfather, Mahlon Bean, kept a notebook, dated 1879-1927, in which he laid out his finances. Entries include 'visit by doctor, ten cents'; 'bought file, 35 cents'; 'filed saw, 20 cents'. Several entries were for a gallon of whiskey, $1.35. The whiskey was needed for medical uses as well as imbibing. It was also used as a medium of exchange. I remember being given a mouthful of whiskey when I had several infected teeth.

My paternal grandmother was Mary Brown, originally from Berryville, just outside of Winchester, Virginia. I was fascinated by the huge turkeys they raised. I didn't know her well, as I was four when she died.

But back to that school on the mountain and the teacher and his student, Orvon and Essye. They married and moved to Moorefield. The area was booming and Dad was hired as a cashier by the local bank. But as you will see, Dad had many jobs and kept learning as he went along. We lived on Elm Street, the main street of the town, in a double house. There was always another family on the other side that paid rent. Orvon and Essye soon began a family.

Family Life

I was the oldest of three brothers and given the unusual name, Wallen. I admit it has been somewhat of a problem, but it was well intentioned. It happened this way: Near the end of the First World War, my father was drafted and sent to Texas. His company was led by a man the soldiers disliked. If they ever went into battle, they grumbled that the lieutenant would be the first casualty. Well, a flu epidemic laid him low and he never returned. His replacement was Lieutenant Wallen.

The men highly respected their new lieutenant for his leadership and would have followed him into battle without question. He certainly made a big impression on my father as he named his first son after him. I like the name but, as I said, it's a problem. I'm often called Walter or Warren and I once received mail addressed W. Allen Bean. I have good reasons for calling my first son Charles Wallen Bean.

My brother Charles was 22 months younger than I, and Rodney five years younger. We hung around together as kids, but Rodney occasionally suffered from convulsions so he got more parental attention. I remember Mother running down the street in a panic with him unconscious in her arms to the doctor's office on the next corner. He was also slow in learning to enunciate properly and was teased into anger when mimicked by Aunt Beulah and my cousin Elizabeth. "I tan toe talk." This did not prevent him from becoming a super athlete, whose biggest rival was my brother Charles. Charles grew up to be six feet three inches tall and some said he could run the football field in ten seconds.

I was completely uncoordinated and not good in sports so it was difficult for me to have such athletic brothers. I had other problems too—I caught more colds, picked up more infections and lived with badly infected teeth. I was also a bed wetter until I was 11 and this chronic problem limited my activities. Under the circumstances, I chose a different path from my brothers and became a bookworm, visiting the library once a week and bringing home piles of books. This avid reading helped me become a top student.

Mother felt that her main function in life was to feed the family. She loved compliments especially after serving her legendary dinner rolls, made from portions of homemade bread, and her other specialty, coconut cake. But Mother had another side too. She was a cultural elitist and made me take piano lessons when I was eight, which continued all the way through high school and into college. My teacher was the judge's wife, Mrs.

Calhoun, who assigned only classical music. I think Mother had dreams of me being a concert pianist but I never developed the required skills and artistry (I was not much good on the piano at all), but nevertheless I developed a love of music which was no doubt nourished by two women—Mother, yes, and my teacher, Alberta Calhoun, who was a true artist. I was at home in their home, my second home.

My family always said grace and had meals together. When we were a little older, we learned to sing:

> *Be present at our table, Lord.*
> *Be here and everywhere adored.*
> *These mercies bless*
> *And grant that we may feast in fellowship with Thee.*

Mother loved to cook and set a fairly formal table, except for breakfast. Breakfast was in the kitchen unless we had company. Mostly we ate in the dining room on her best china, Nortake, the Azalea pattern. She purchased the early place settings with coupons and always washed these precious dishes very carefully by hand. Mother did the serving and sometimes overdid it with the helpings, encouraging us to eat even when we were stuffed. I was keenly aware that she expected compliments and felt hurt if she didn't get them. My brother Rodney and I each inherited a 92-piece set from her collection.

Both my parents hoped their sons would develop skills in public speaking, which my father felt he lacked. He always had a fear that he would say something in public and use improper English. He was self-educated beyond his years of formal training and very intelligent, but he worried about making mistakes that might make him seem lacking.

In spite of not always meeting my parent's expectations, I had an enviable childhood. I loved swimming, fishing, exploring and visiting relatives. We were free spirits in a way that today's structured kids could only dream about.

The house next to ours was the oldest house in town, a log cabin that had been covered by clapboards long ago. As a boy I remember the very old lady who sat in the sun on the sidewalk scratching her head until it was raw because it itched. Mother said she needed her hair washed, and that was a problem in those days. Most houses had a well. We had to heat water on the kitchen stove for bathing so we could have a bath or shampoo in the tub only once a week. This ritual usually took place on Saturday night in preparation for us attending church on Sunday dressed in our best clothes.

Lottie Laken lived on the other side of the log cabin house. Her father was building a nice-looking, two-story house. The roof was on and the inner structure was completed, as well as the kitchen, when he died suddenly. The house was never finished. There were no clapboards and the innards were exposed to the weather. I watched it turn brown over the years until Lottie's mother died, and then she died. Not until then did someone buy and finish it.

My brothers and I spent many a summer day swimming in a section of the South Fork River just back of town, in a place where the river pooled about six feet deep—a true swimming hole. The big attraction was a large rope that hung from a sycamore tree, and we raced to our jumping off spot where you could swing out over the water and drop about eight feet (yes, into six feet of water). On warm afternoons, we played and dove for objects and stayed and stayed and stayed. Dr. Brooks' son, who was ten years older than I, taught me to swim. My complete lack of coordination didn't help so the best I could do was a crawl, but even that had its limitations. I could not master the flutter kick, which is pretty essential to the crawl so I would splash around in my own way, but I could probably have saved myself if necessary.

Fishing was something else—it was the one sport I was good at. I often brought my casting rod and some spinners and fished up the river with my friend, Scotty Reynolds, which made it all the more fun. Down the river from the swimming hole was Kirkendahl Island, a flood plain that contained a number of potholes gouged out by the floods. They were rich in water life, fish and frogs, ducks and nesting birds—our true nature sanctuary. We even attempted to build a cabin out of driftwood, and I do mean "attempted." Along the way, I acquired a fine casting rod made of steel and the first level winder reel in town. I learned to cast well enough to put a lure under the over-hanging branches jutting out from the shore so I could get a strike from a lurking bass.

Appalachian Food

With the first frost announcing a new, colder season, the gallon crock was set out to mix the buckwheat cakes we'd have every winter morning. A precious bit of yeast added to a cup of buckwheat flour began fermentation, and then the crock would sit on the back of the kitchen stove on a plate which caught the overflow. At Uncle Jake's the crock, a 40-gallon copper kettle, provided batter to feed a family of four through the winter and still have enough "starter" to ferment the next batch. We ate the pancakes with butter, honey, jams and gravy. Once a year we went to the Buckwheat Festival in Buckhannon.

Ham was frequently on the menu. We did not raise pigs but Father would buy several hams and sugar-cure them. A mixture of salt, brown sugar and spices were slapped on the ham, then wrapped in brown paper, sewed up in a bag and left hanging for six months in a smoke house. We often found a little mold on the ham when it was opened up, but that was not a problem.

Mother canned fruits and vegetables with gusto. We had lots of applesauce and apple pie, but Father's favorite dessert was lemon pie with a top crust. For Sunday dinner, we almost always had honey-fried chicken, mashed potatoes, fruit or lemon pie and, of course, Mother's dinner rolls. We also socked down plenty of homemade breads and cornbread.

Meat often came from the forests and fields—rabbit, squirrel, ground hog, turkey, deer. The men were more likely to do the cooking if the meat was wild—we called it the South Branch Diet. My father and his friends went on several trips to the "sinks," an area dotted with small caves and sink holes, and amid the tall grass and wild strawberries were hundreds of groundhogs. The men took their most powerful rifles and competed in making kills at the greatest distance. The meat of young groundhogs was highly prized and so was venison, but the cutting of the forests reduced the deer population. In the remote sections of the woods, however, hunters were abundant. The Hines family owned a thousand acres of tree-covered land and they could kill one deer each year as compensation for damage to crops. I remember asking Orion Hines how they could grow such large parsnips and turnips without the deer eating them. He answered, "They wouldn't dare," and you could see murder in his eye.

Farm Ponds

Farm ponds are in vogue today, as if they were something new, but the old farmers of West Virginia built such ponds on their own property long ago. Only the farm pond offers a continuous source of protein. Surprisingly, there is only one natural pond in the state of West Virginia. Trout Pond is fed by two large springs of water at Wardensville, near the home of Aunt Beulah and Uncle Lee.

The productivity of the homemade farm pond is truly amazing. One need only supply it with sunfish and bass and let it be. Food for the sunfish comes from the insect larvae in the bottom of the pond as well as from myriad sources outside. The bass, which feed primarily on the sunfish, can reach mammoth proportions and still manage to swallow anything up to half its size.

In the 1960s, long after I left home, Dad built a farm pond on our property, taking advantage of a wet spot in the narrow meadow in the upper end of the hay field. He hired a bulldozer and put it to work damning up the stream that gave us water except in the driest of summers. However, our pond was never dry. A dozen or so bass will thrive in this barn-size pond and the largest one is the king. The king bass is almost always the first one to be caught in an unfished pond because the king goes after the bait. If a smaller bass should try for it, he may be eaten first.

In 1976, a pair of beavers took up residence in our pond. They had been reintroduced after having been absent for several years. Apparently when a litter of kits become mature and the parents are ready to mate again, the kits are driven off. So it is in the world of nature.

Games

We played many games in the back yard, most of them made up. One was unique but probably not kind. Swarms of bats constantly flew around our house, as they liked to feast on the confetti of insects. The bats would swoop under a grape vine, fly up over a wire fence and glide under the limb of the walnut tree that my father planted when I was born. Our weapon of choice was a baseball bat and we had zero hits with many times at bat over the course of two summers. Then when we learned that bats had the ability to use echoes to dodge objects we came up with another plan. On the garage was a wire rug beater about a foot wide, and we knew a weapon when we saw one. The rug beater did the trick and brought down more than a few bats.

"Stop. Stop this minute," Mother yelled when she found out what we were doing. "Bats are valuable for eating insects. Leave them alone."

She was right. We had to surrender at our moment of victory.

There was a danger in Moorefield I haven't mentioned. Young men would often come from the city with their guns looking for deer. They had very high-powered rifles and were not as experienced or as careful as they should have been. It was, in fact, very dangerous for them and for us. Every year we had one or two fatalities.

Moorefield was a town that tolerated, even prized, trickery on Halloween, unless it got out of hand. One man found his car out of town, pushed there (not driven) by a gang of boys—this was considered extreme. One of our more benign pranks was the act of swapping short garden hoses for long ones half way across town. Most of the residents took it in stride but one old gentleman named Willard, who lived three houses down the street from me, became enraged when a green ball the size of a grapefruit was thrown on his porch.

Willard was wildly eccentric and liked his booze. If one of us yelled his name out loud—Will-l-l-lard—he'd curse like a trooper. One evening, as we were tramping home from downtown, he stepped out from behind the elm tree in his front yard and held up a knife. Trying to scare us, I guess, but he was just old and drunk and pathetic.

About a month later, however, frigid air swooped in on us from the north and dropped an unexpected foot of snow. I was trudging home at dusk from a school program when I saw this peculiar dark spot in the snow near Willard's house. I moved closer to investigate and it was Willard himself! Drunk again, he had slipped on the icy undercoat and hit his head. Unable to get up, he had stopped struggling and lay there half-buried, covered with heavy snow, as still as a body in a coffin. I pushed and pulled, dragged and carried him into the house and covered him with blankets. He came back to life. Ever after, he greeted me with a smile. But he was lucky. Had I not seen that ominous, dark spot, he would have frozen to death.

Chapter 2

Fanny

Fanny was a black woman who came to our house once a week to scrub floors and wash dishes—she was not allowed to prepare food. Housecleaning earned her fifty cents a day. We thought of her as a member of the family. I was just a little kid and she scared me at first because she had a fang, a sharp eyetooth that moved up and down when she talked. I thought she would kill me with that tooth. Later I learned that the fang was a result of malnutrition.

Back home, she had six children and her husband was long gone. She lived near the railroad tracks in a one-room shack made of crating from the railroad. Negroes went to the black school, a structure that looked like a house, and it went up to the eighth grade. Fanny made sure her children got to school, but that's where education ended for most black people. Besides the fang, she was crippled with one leg very much shorter than the other. Her legs were deformed because she had TB as a child. Fanny loved to sing while she worked and I loved to listen to her songs. Sometimes my friends and I sat on the edge of the road that led to her church so we could hear their singing. Fanny was the first black person I knew, and though there were limits, she was my friend.

Well before the Civil War, southern-style plantations grew up in the rich soil of the South Branch Valley. Five of these plantations were maintained by slaves. At the end of the Civil War, the McNeil family alone freed a whopping 99 slaves. These people continued as sharecroppers with contracts, farming the owner's land for the next 70 years. A caste system evolved to maintain control over these former slaves, but the sharecropping business ended during the Second World War. Mechanical equipment for planting and harvesting made the sharecropper obsolete. (In the 1950s, blacks fled to the growing cities. Washington D.C. grew from ten percent black to fifty.)

A quarter of the people in Moorefield were black, a population directly descended from these slaves. Moorefield would have been at home in Georgia in its social structure. Both had a caste system in full sway designed to keep the black man in his place.

Another black who made a deep impression on me was Lou, a huge man with an operatic voice and kind demeanor. When the farmers came into town on Saturday night, they would get him in a corner and tell him ribald jokes with racial slurs, demanding that he laugh. If he didn't laugh, they said they would kill him. You can bet your life, he laughed. One night I overheard a conversation in which a friend asked Lou why he laughed. "I gotta laugh, I gotta laugh," he said, as if his life depended on it. There was an enduring pain in that laughter. I can hear it now, 75 years later. I feel it and see it—the pain in that laughter.

You always called a black person by a first name. I did not know that Fanny and Lou had last names. I learned later that Fanny was Fanny Ford. And I knew George Washington Brooks, the Boy Scout cook who taught me to fish. He died at 24 because he had no medical care. Only one doctor in town would treat black people. And if a black came into a white Christian church, there would be an uproar. We weren't too Christian in those days.

The greatest source of danger was the poorest of white men, those at the bottom of the social ladder. They rode at night, led the KKK, lynched. In the past, they were poor because they had to compete with black slave labor and that history fed their grievances into the present day.

In the black part of town there were no facilities—no sewers, no electricity and no garbage collection. The people seemed to wear rags, which the whites might have given them. On the way to one of my favorite fishing spots in the fork, I had to pass through a section of the black community and remember seeing a little black girl playing in the street. When she bent over, I could see the insignia of a popular flour company written across the back of her pants. Their logo was "Good as Gold." Her pants were made out of a flour sack.

By the time I reached high school, segregation was given a kinder take. It was now "separate but equal." Separate, yes, but Moorefield and the nation, for that matter, had a way to go on the "equal." There was enormous pressure on whites to conform to the disrespect of blacks. I told racial jokes too until I was old enough to realize what I was doing. In the book "Anna Karenina," Leo Tolstoy says it well: "There are no conditions of life to which a man cannot get accustomed, especially if he sees them accepted by everyone around him." I sensed something was wrong even when I was quite young. But later, when I truly knew it was wrong, the pressure was there to keep quiet. I had the feeling that if you defended blacks, the townspeople would kill you too. It was more than a feeling.

My father was a complicated soul in this regard and tread a fine line. He was very democratic. He didn't violate the caste system but he clearly felt that blacks "didn't get their share," and he conveyed this to me. I was very influenced by him.

Visitors

Our house was always warm and welcoming. Visits by extended family members were weekly events. Aunts and uncles spent their vacation time in our house, which sometimes amounted to weeks, and family reunions were especially common in the summer time. I remember piles of food rising on the table as people arrived with arms full. Though she had left school herself, Mother was a firm believer in education, and she encouraged family members to continue their education. Few of the Valley towns had high schools, but Moorefield did. In 1932, my uncle Johnny (Arno) Reed, only four years older than I, lived with us so he could attend high school. Several other relatives lived here for the same reason. As you might guess, Mother was the one everyone looked up to, the problem solver for the entire family. But then, that was the role she played growing up with all those brothers and sisters.

Her father's wealth had allowed her brother Tom, my oldest uncle, to attend medical school and it was a great day for all when he earned his degree. His first practice was in a coal-mining town of 1500 people, and he was paid by the mining company. The nearest hospital was 75 miles away. On one occasion he had to amputate to save a miner's life. Later he practiced in Charleston, West Virginia where he became a kidney specialist and president of the West Virginia Medical Association. Uncle Tom, the doctor, was a frequent visitor at my home and he told us that Mother was his favorite sister. When his five-year-old daughter died of leukemia, it was a family tragedy that haunts us to this day.

Another visitor was Mother's oldest brother Virgil, a pharmacist in Pittsburgh. Married to Anna from Paw Paw, West Virginia, they had a daughter with long red curls that hung in ringlets to her shoulders. Many a summer vacation they spent in my home.

Meanwhile, my grandfather's premature death ended the educational opportunities for the rest of his family. On my father's side, there were no opportunities even to begin. Relatives on both sides of the family ended up going to Washington D.C. for jobs.

Today my mind is still full of aunts and uncles and grannies who populated my life and gave it color and shape, leaving me with memories that burst into life at odd moments, like flowers.

Uncle Lee and Aunt Beulah

Many of the larger family reunions were held at the farm of Uncle Lee Heltzel and Aunt Beulah who lived on Pine Ridge, about 25 miles out of town. I will always associate Uncle Lee with ice cream memories, the kind a kid never forgets. He made ice cream using ice he had stored in the icehouse. It formed on a nearby pond, was cut into chunks and stored in sawdust. The cream was from Guernsey cows, the richest cream of all. (The pigs did not make out as well; they got the skim milk.) The freezer held two gallons and the boys—my brothers, my cousins and I—were in charge of turning the handle until we could turn no more, and then the big guys were brought in. The strongest adults had to finish it off. After the churning, it sat for an hour to harden. My uncle, who was six feet tall and always carried a cane, would open the freezer and fill a dish as high as a mountain and then he'd laugh and say "Eat it or I'll beat you with my cane."

Aunt Beulah was a teacher and taught first grade in Wardensville for 40 years. Uncle Lee made his living as an engineer, businessman and farmer, raising mostly hens. They had one child, Elizabeth, the only member of my family I did not like but more about her later. When I was visiting, I helped Uncle Lee gather close to a thousand eggs a day, and he earned eight cents a dozen. He and Aunt Beulah fed their animals all they could eat, from appetizers to dessert. Their riding horses were too fat to run. For that matter, Uncle Lee was a fatty himself, eating three eggs for breakfast and downing ice cream faster than the kids. Life changed for him after he had a heart attack and was put on a diet.

Uncle Lee loved trout and persuaded me to visit frequently so I could catch him some trout. The state stocked Trout Pond and the farm ponds with bass and sunfish. The first time I fished in the stream I caught six small brook trout, which was half the limit. Uncle Lee gave me a tip: If I worked my way through the brush to each pond above the springs, I could catch the biggest trout in the pond. But, he cautioned, I would have to wait a half hour after disturbing the pond before they would feed again. He was right. I brought home twelve trout the next day and the day after. When he died of a second heart attack when I was fourteen, he still had some trout in the freezer.

Aunt Verdi and Uncle Jake

My father's sister, Aunt Verdi, married Jacob Heishman and they lived ten miles from Moorefield on an eleven-acre farm on top of Simon Bean Mountain. She was his second wife. They were subsistence farmers and never made more than $300 a year, but they managed to raise three children. We visited them often. My father made life easier for them by buying them their first battery radio, which they listened to only on Sunday to hear a sermon. Actually the battery went dead before they really learned to use it.

At Jake and Verdi's house, there were rules. Two turns on the bar of homemade soap and that was all. He enforced the rule because the soap had to last until the next summer when a new batch was made. Secondly, the cistern water that drained off the tin roof had no minerals in it. You could not get the soap off without using a lot of water and it had to go from the stream to the big iron stove that held the washing tubs.

Many cooperative activities were held at the farm and making apple butter was one of them. My uncle cultivated a "wolf river" apple, the size of a grapefruit. On apple butter day, the fire under his 40-gallon copper pot was lit and had to be fed constantly. We also had to stir the apple butter without interruption to keep it from burning. A ladle attached to a four-foot pole made it possible to stir without getting burned. The boys did much of the stirring.

One summer my uncle wanted to clear a piece of his land across the highway on a steep slope, land covered with large rocks and rich soil. That summer I was introduced to the Grub Hoe. My father had told me how hard it was to clear land covered with trees. The roots had to be grubbed out, which was back breaking labor. It was all too true. Well, we planted corn and it came up just fine, but two enemies awaited—the crows and apparently me. The crows pulled up the seedling, on the one hand, and I inadvertently let a rock get started down that hill and it took out a whole row of corn. My uncle was not very happy.

When Jake and Verdi became too infirm to farm their eleven acres, my father bought the farm for $500, which was twice its value, on the condition that ownership be delayed until they died. My father was incredibly generous that way. Jake and Verdi are long gone now, but I see them clearly. Uncle Jake was quite religious and said prayers at mealtime. When we were about to leave, we'd say, "See you next time." His response was always "God willing."

Uncle Jake had a son with his first wife who lived in Pennsylvania and he drove the large trucks that delivered new cars to dealers. The only time I ever met him is when he came to his dad's funeral and took back with him all the best furniture, the Edison phonograph, and some 200 recordings worth a fortune. I believe the items were willed to him.

My father's mother lived the last fifteen years of her life with Aunt Verdi and Uncle Jake. She died at 85, when I was four, so I have few memories of her. But the family stories about her are vivid. She became a recluse after her husband died and rarely left her room in the back bedroom on the second floor. Family members said that whenever an able-bodied person visited the house, she got sick and went to bed. I guess that was the only way she could cope. By not coping.

The other mystery person in my family was Uncle Grover, my father's brother, diagnosed as mentally ill at 18, and confined to the state mental hospital. He died in his late 30s. Though I heard family stories about him, I did not know him. He was the ghost in the attic.

Uncle Cleland and Aunt Effie

Uncle Cleland and Aunt Effie lived in Sligo, Maryland, on a dairy farm my uncle managed. They had two daughters, Irma Lee and June. We liked to visit them and their menagerie of animals. The chickens were kept in a large enclosure ruled by a huge red rooster. When I was eight I decided to slip into the cage and catch a chicken. The rooster thought better of that. When I was thoroughly inside, it attacked and pecked me just under the eye hard enough to draw blood. Believe me, I did not try that again.

The farm was adjacent to the Chevy Chase golf course with a putting green next to the house. Uncle Cleland's bulldog discouraged everyone from climbing the fence to retrieve any balls that landed in our yard, so we were assured a steady supply of balls. When I was 12, my uncle gave me a pail of golf balls and a club. I remember taking a swing alongside the house and slicing it. I watched guiltily as it raced through the big window and shattered the glass. Father warned me against a repeat performance and when he confronted yet another broken window, I never saw the club and ball again, though I looked high and low. Years later, when we broke through the brick foundation of the house to enlarge an area for a furnace, there lay the infamous golf balls and club, rusted by the passage of time.

Aunt Olga and Uncle Henry

Aunt Olga was my mother's sister and Uncle Henry was her second husband. She returned to Needmore from Washington, D.C. after marrying him. Henry was overweight, partly from overeating and partly from drinking beer. He had a deep, full-bellied laugh, worked hard and took good care of Olga as she developed a form of dementia, today known as Alzheimer's disease. I remember how she was always frightened to be alone. They, too, lived on about eleven acres of land, the old farmstead where Dad kept some of his bees. When the gas company began drilling in the area, they made a find on Henry's land. Eventually the land was used as a gas storage area to cover high peak usage.

Uncle Johnny and Aunt Margaret

When our family lived at the mill (coming up next), my uncle Johnny (Arno) Reed lived with us so he could go to high school. Just four years older than I, he played games with us and we teased him unmercifully. Several times we tried to put onion juice in his mashed potatoes just before he was going out on a date. He always took these antics in good spirits, which was why he was so popular with everyone.

After he graduated, he moved to Washington, D.C. and drove a taxi, then built up his own fleet of taxis. He accomplished much, including marrying Aunt Margaret from Massachusetts. Margaret worked for an Air Force general and flew all over the world. She had won a national speed contest as a typist and she addressed an envelope with such a flourish— like an artist. A regal lady, she was the first Catholic I ever knew. I was impressed by her loyalty to the church as she drove 35 miles to Keyser every Sunday to attend Mass. Under her influence, Johnny became Catholic. They had two children, a boy and a girl, and were frequent visitors to our house.

One of the family stories features Johnny and the professional dancer, Eleanor Powell. Whenever she was dancing in Washington, she hired Johnny to drive her around in a cab for a couple of hours so she could rest and sleep. There were rumors that my Aunt Margaret was jealous but no one recalls her complaining.

Uncle Junior

Junior was another mystery uncle I knew little about until he came to live in our home for a year to get over his addiction to alcohol. He had been a gunner on a B17 bomber during the war and came home with a drinking problem. Junior was Mother's brother and she talked him into living with us. The entire family knew about his problem and were united in helping him gain control. Living with us actually worked. Years later, he was asked why it worked when everything else he tried had failed. He would laugh and say, "I would have to face my sister again if I didn't get cured!" In reflection, this was further evidence of something I came to believe in: the power of small groups, this time a family. To live in my family was to belong.

Bean Settlement

Now that you know a few of the relatives, I will give a quick history of the family. On both sides, the family stems from that great uprooting 200 years ago in England. The English kings decided they could make more money running sheep than they could in renting land to farmers. They evicted their tenants in a brutal fashion by canceling their contracts and burning their villages. They succeeded in driving people out, among them, the Beans.

The Bean family fled to America and wandered up the Potomac River into the mountains to establish Bean Settlement. Their farms were carved out of the top of the mountains. There were marriages, births, deaths. There was land to be tamed, jobs to do, kids to send to school. The mountain is still referred to as Simon Bean Mountain, where we began in America.

Eventually the Bean Settlement community developed a primitive telephone system that served about 20 families. The switchboard was located in the Hines' house, and its system was far more complicated than a walkie-talkie, as it had to climb mountains and reach into remote hollows. Each subscriber had a number of rings that conveyed a signal for a call and, believe me, people were happy to hear the phone ring. The telephone was a welcome resource for an isolated area where houses were miles apart. There was a danger, however. Wooden inserts wrapped in aluminum foil connected the various components. Lightning strikes were frequent and, over the years, I heard many frightening stories of how a bolt of lightning rolled out of the speaker, crossed the room and zoomed down a corner pipe. It became clear that telephones should not be used during storms, and when a lightning storm ended, an all-clear signal meant that everyone was OK and life could go on as usual—it was safe to use the phone.

I have two ledgers recording the business activity of a country store in Inkerman, W.Va., about four miles from where my father was born. On the flyleaf of the older book, penciled in my grandfather's bold hand, is its name: the "Mahlon L. Bean Book," which is the only time his name occurs in the ledgers. However, his brother Simon Bean who lived next door to him has dozens of transactions. (Simon's house was the only one in town with brick walls.) The ledger begins in 1879 and runs to 1924. Its pages were assigned to individual customers and used for calculations and entries. Many of the transactions have to do with the care and dispensation of horses. The first page informs us of Mahlon's business:

Dec. 10, paid to mail carrier, 20 cents
Colt taken to Lobs M., May 11, 1896
Colt taken away, July 26, 1896
Taken colt away from here, Oct. 17

On the second page, among other notations:
Note to Wesley Bean, March 1889 for $55, settled with Simon Bean
Note to Wesley Bean, August 27, 1889 for $100
Simon Bean bought colt for $30 January 17, 1890

An advertisement for the country store uses a direct attack:

Clothing for the naked, Glasses for the blind
Shoes for the barefooted, Gloves that are lined.
Curtains for the windows/ Shoestrings and laces;
Lamps, Wicks and Oil/ To light the dark places
Dried fruits, canned goods/ Everything to eat;
Caps for the head and socks for the feet
Calico of the finest/ That never fails
Woolen Goods for dresses/ Ribbons for old maids
Tobacco for menfolk/ Hats for the ladies

Chapter 3

The J.B. Natwick Lumber Company

In 1930, when I was eight, my life changed dramatically when Dad was offered a new job. The J.B. Natwick Lumber Company owned 30,000 acres in the headwaters of the Potomac River and Dad was hired to be the bookkeeper. We moved from the town to the mill. His office was on the second floor of the storage warehouse and our apartment took up the remaining space. In other words, our apartment was not the nice house we left. We were housed in the warehouse containing supplies for the operation up the south fork in the headwaters of the Potomac River. Mother was a little unhappy with the apartment because there was no closet space. My parents bought a very large closet, which we dubbed THE THING, and it was big enough to play in.

The site was a lumber mill when it first opened in 1920; it closed in 1929 and reopened the next year as Natwick Hardwood Lumber Company. Dad worked for the lumber company for ten years. Every day the train took the workers to the lumber camp, a 28-mile trip.

The ten houses that made up the town were owned by the company and the rent was included in the wages of the lumbermen; so, too, with our apartment. All the houses were painted red and a flowerbed made of old automobile tires had similar flowers planted inside each one. An employee did not dare offend the boss. If he quit or was fired, he not only lost his income, he also lost his community.

I remember several incidents that made a big impression on me. The superintendent was a mean-spirited, profane man I would not want to meet in a dark alley. One evening he pushed an employee up against a fence and swore at him for half an hour. Insult followed insult. Mother said to us we must never use that kind of language, as it was evidence of being uneducated. A Christian didn't use such words.

This incident no doubt was related to an earlier event involving the employee, the night watchman. He guarded the town at night armed with a pistol. One night he came to work drunk and went on a rampage, which was unusual because he was not known to be a drinker. He got into an argument with the superintendent, broke the windshield of his car, and walked down the street firing his pistol. My father, who was notified of the trouble, found the watchman and persuaded him to surrender his pistol. In fact, they were good friends and the watchman trusted my father.

I overheard their conversation. The watchman said he had been drinking whiskey and this explained his bad behavior. He said he was not a regular drinker and this craziness wouldn't happen again. Apparently my father defended him with the boss and it saved the watchman his job. But he still got a dressing down later on, the likes of which I've never seen.

One of Dad's worst days occurred when he could not balance his books by one cent. This seems unbelievable to me today.

The mill was on the edge of town and I remember walking to school on the railroad tracks, trying to see how far I could keep my balance on the rail itself without falling off. Not long after moving to this more isolated place, I became afraid of a big German Shepherd dog that regularly had seizures. He'd go into spasms, jerk his body around, froth at the mouth and bite his tongue until it bled. The owner would quickly call him over (the dog obeyed) and hold him down until the spell was over. There was nowhere to hide from this beast—he seemed to be everywhere.

One day I experienced more than a few moments of terror when I was on the porch alone and four screen doors stood between me and safety indoors. When the dog started toward me, I ran screaming for each door and found all of them locked. For years afterward, that German Shepherd chased me in a host of nightmare dreams. I did not get over the dreams until graduate school when our good friends, the Gemmells, got a puppy named Houdini and he was nothing but friendly. After ten years, we moved back to town. Surprisingly, I do not remember much about moving back.

The company was wiped out (after I left home) by the Great Fire that took place on April 1, 1945, causing about $400,000 worth of damage. This was quite a bit of money for those days. The Moorefield Examiner said the fire began around 8 a.m. and was so ferocious that five communities, some from 30 miles away, sent their fire trucks to assist. The fire was a wipe-out, taking the main buildings, the tool shed, the apartment building and office where we lived (as well as "The Thing"), immense amounts of stored hardwood flooring and lumber, a railroad box car, a loaded dry kiln and a gondola. Had the wind been from a different direction, it would have burned the entire town of Moorefield.

It could not have been easy for Father to work for a lumber company. He loved trees. He was far more interested in growing trees than in cutting them down. He planted a black walnut tree in the backyard to celebrate my birth and nurtured every black walnut he found on the farm. Altogether he planted hundreds of them. He also planted pine seedlings even though they had little chance of thriving as the deer got them first. He mourned the loss of the most important tree, the chestnut tree. Chestnuts were a food source for wild animals and a daily diet for pigs. Nevertheless, he had to make a living and since we were surrounded by mountains, the money was in lumber.

There's a rhythm to the growth of a forest that I observed growing up in the Appalachians. I saw fire up there, I saw floods, but most of all I saw the exploitation of those forests by man. Trees can survive the fires and floods, but not always the greed of man. After hundreds of years of growth, the trees were harvested for lumber. The Natwick Lumber Company operated in the days when there were no restrictions on lumbering operations. The company took everything, and sometimes it was hard to look at the debris that was left behind. Father was an advocate of selective cutting but the companies felt they couldn't make enough money unless they bulldozed everything in sight.

The big trees went to Moorefield to be sawed into lumber, and then the boards were piled into stacks 30 feet high. Wet lumber will warp so it took a year of drying before it could be sold. Other parts of trees were made into railroad ties. The remainder of the wood was hauled away to Piedmont and made into paper.

The hillsides were denuded. The roots of the trees, the accumulated peat moss and tree limbs littered about, burned on for 20 years or so. The exposed soil generated floods and, over the years, the soil became ten feet thick in parts of the South Branch Valley. Although this process slowed down the re-growth of the forest, the new trees gradually took root. In rich soil the foliage thrived.

If the trees have a rhythm in the mountains, so do the wildlife—bear, deer, turkeys. They come and go, often depending on forest growth. Black bears roamed about but I kept out of their way. On one occasion, however, several woodsmen captured a young bear and caged him and he became an attraction, especially for children. One day a man was teasing it and stuck his finger through the wire. The bear bit it off. The bear was probably miserable living in that cage and knew an opportunity when he saw one.

As the new forest grew, so did the deer herds. They grew so numerous they destroyed the apple orchards on top of the mountains. Things changed from year to year. One year we would buy apples at the orchards and they were all top-of-the-tree apples, bright and beautiful from the ample sunshine. The next year the deer herds would have eaten every apple they could reach. When the herd was at its height, some 4,000 bucks were killed in a two-week hunting season. We actually counted 200 dead deer in a 30-mile stretch of highway. We teasingly called a cousin who'd had a previous run-in with a deer to ask whether he'd traveled this road recently since corpses littered the roadside. When the trees got too tall for the deer to reach the foliage, the herds began to diminish.

Wild turkey are in this picture too. They flourish when they can feed on the young trees and as a result are now the more numerous wildlife. On my last trip home, a Tom turkey flew up and hit my windshield, nearly causing me to crash. The forest in that area had come through a full cycle and, it seemed, touched all living things.

Father had access to numerous baby animals. When the trees were cut many animal nests were destroyed, and some of these little wild ones ended up as pets. We obtained a pair of baby raccoons in this manner and they were safe enough for me to play with until they became adults. Actually Father and his friend Orion Hines built a cage to raise them for the fur market—hunting and trapping were a way of life for the Appalachian families. One day I was feeding the raccoons, who were nearly adults by this time. The male raccoon loved chewing and I had just given him half a stick of teaberry gum which he chewed for half a minute, then started looking for more.

Restless and tired, I made the mistake of leaning against the wire on the front of the cage and my left hand was resting against it. The raccoon suddenly attacked, biting me through the wire. I screamed in pain. My attempts to pull loose didn't work as the raccoon kept on biting and I kept on screaming. Father came running and quickly opened the cage door, grabbed the animal by the throat and choked it until it let go. My wound was deep, right down to the bone, and I nearly developed blood poisoning. The attack changed the personality of the raccoon. If I approached the cage, it would charge the wire and growl at me. You can bet I lost interest in having raccoons as pets and gladly sent these two off to the fur market.

Making a Living

Besides the tree business, raising cattle is big here in the valley too, especially buying and selling calves to be fattened on those rich fields of clover. Clover-fed beef brought a higher price than corn-fattened beef. Calves were produced by the small subsistence farmer like my Uncle Jake. No factory farming in Moorefield.

Dairy farming was a family operation too and helped keep up the calf supply. In order to produce milk, the cow had to be bred each year. My friend, Don Miley, lived on a large farm in the valley where his father bought and sold calves. Here I learned a few facts of life. He had expensive prize bulls whose duties were to breed with cows on neighboring farms. The bulls were trucked to the farm that had a cow in heat, or sometimes the cows were trucked to the Miley farm. One year during a rabies epidemic, one of his bulls was bitten by a rabid fox and had to be put down. The whole town knew about it and considered it a great loss.

The Miley's barn was huge and we kids were allowed to play in the hay. Un-baled hay was a fire danger and many local barns had full haylofts. Huge flocks of pigeons roosted at night up in the eaves. Their enormous excretion would wet down the hay, which was a hazard because the moisture could cause spontaneous combustion and set the barn on fire.

Every farm family had its flock of chickens, which ate grains and scraps from the dinner table. The "chicken hawk," not to be confused with a chicken, was despised for taking a meal now and then. The chickens were on their own, fat and unconfined. When chicken houses were added to the buildings, my father believed it was the beginning of the end of a good tasting chicken. Ask any West Virginia farmer—chickens need to grow muscles before going in the pot, and they do it chasing grasshoppers in the barnyard. In Moorefield, we had a tradition of inviting our Protestant preacher for Sunday dinner, and we served chicken, of course.

One of the ways a teenager could earn money was to cut down the great oak trees and trim the bark, which was bundled up and hauled to the tannery on the South Fork of the Potomac River. The tannery was a nasty business but somebody had to do it, I suppose. The tanning of hides into leather required the acid found in oak bark. That's right, oak bark. A residue of this thick, black fluid was called "ooze" and was stored in holding lagoons until a time of high water, then the gates were opened and the lagoons emptied into the river. The high water assured minimal damage to the river ecology. In August of 1945, when the water was low, a break in the wall of the lagoon allowed the ooze to poison the river. For about a mile down river, all the fish were killed. What a mess! The worst thing was to see several bushels of dead fish on the riverbanks.

The pumping of water from the river into the town filtering system was abruptly stopped. By Friday, all town water was cut off, causing the Thompson Mahogany plant to abruptly close and workers at the Rockingham Poultry Cooperative to haul water to finish the day's orders. All the townspeople suffered hardships since they lost their water without warning. Eventually the fire departments of Moorefield and Petersburg got together and laid a hose long enough to reach clean water above the polluted area so they could fill the town reservoir. Though the high water from heavy rains on Saturday and Sunday did much to clear out the channel of the South Fork, nothing could bring back the dead fish. Sad to say, in Moorefield, sewers still empty into the river just above where the town pumps its water supply.

Moorefield had an excellent volunteer fire department but the farms were scattered about the countryside and could not be quickly reached. By the time the alarm went off, the fire might be raging ten miles away and there wasn't a prayer of saving the barn. Another hindrance was a deep, three-foot drop in the driveway from the firehouse. The siren was actually on the bank building a block away and it screamed so loud, it could wake up the dead. Several of the firemen were designated drivers and the first one to arrive drove. One night a fireman was racing toward the station, half-dressed. While putting his suspenders over his shoulders, his slipper went sailing about ten feet in front of him. He accelerated, caught the slipper in mid-air and kept on going without missing a beat. I always had a fear the fire truck would come zipping down that lane too fast, fail to make the turn into the street, and come straight into our living room.

One summer the farmers awarded prizes for a "pest killing." On the list of pests were rats, mice, pigeons, starlings and "skillpots," a common turtle that lived in the river and farm ponds. Feral cats were on the list too, former barn cats who went wild and became a danger to the flocks of backyard chickens. Don and I won a prize that summer because he had a big red dog who liked nothing better than digging for hours to destroy the undergrounds nests of mice and rats. They became visible when the shocks of corn were hauled off to the corncribs. That day we turned in hundreds of tails of rats and mice. We each won a pint of ice cream from Friddle's drug store, the first time I had a whole pint to myself. I ate it all, of course. Ice cream was 15 cents a pint.

Occasionally we got cold treats if we put in some time working for the milk station, which was located at the railroad depot, four blocks from my house. Each day, dairy farmers loaded their milk and cream in five and ten gallon cans onto pickup trucks, then headed off to the milk station. Here the milk and cream were frozen so they would not sour on the long railroad trip to Cumberland, Maryland. Occasionally, if we were helping load or unload, the man in charge would thank us by breaking off frozen chunks of cream. We filled our mouths with this frigid, Appalachian treat that froze our tongues and lungs and made the heat on those long summer days almost bearable.

Neighbors and Townspeople

One reason I was a poor athlete was that I had constant infections in my mouth, which means I got to know the dentist, Dr. Harmon, pretty well. He was the husband of the church organist at Duffy Memorial Methodist Church and the center of much town gossip. Dr. Harmon had a drinking problem resulting in binges in which he disappeared for days.

One time, Carl Bean was sent to the dentist to have all his teeth filled, as he had many cavities. Dr. Harmon was known to drill and fill as long as his patient could sit still. He ended up filling all of Carl's teeth in one sitting and when Carl got to the door, he turned around and said, "When I get big enough, I'm gonna come back here and beat the hell out of you."

For several years, when the dentist had a couple of drinks in him, you could hear him in town yelling, "Hey, when are you coming back here to beat me up?" It all ended when Carl died in the war.

Dr. Harmon's wife did not trust him and for good reason; he was not a particularly trustworthy man. He hired the sexiest girl in the class as his office assistant. The dentist's wife made quite a fuss, and she and the girl became enemies. She even warned her never to walk past their house. When the young lady strolled by one evening, Mrs. Harmon hit her in the head with a Coke bottle. The girl sued and collected $10,000. At all social affairs after that, Dr. Harmon would introduce his wife by saying he paid $10,000 for her.

An endearing character of my childhood was uncle Calvin Swisher. He was not really my uncle but he and my father had been in the army together and developed a lifelong friendship. He lived in Pittsburgh and became a wealthy business owner, then lost everything in the Great Depression. The only thing he had left was a little mountain farm near Needmore, West Virginia. His wife had broken under their heavy loss and had gone quite insane. He took tender care of her.

Uncle Cal had no children so he loved to have us with him, and he liked to fish as much as I did. One day he told me there were some big turtles in the backwater ponds on the Harper farm near Petersburg just waiting for us to catch them. I got permission to go off on this adventure and we arrived at the ponds, set out four sections of heavy line with four hooks and baited them with the cheek of a cow, the toughest beef, then left the lines overnight. Sure enough, the next day we found four turtles. The two small ones were put in separate barrels 'til they were big enough for the pot and two were plump enough for dinner.

Since Uncle Cal was a good cook and we were often guests at his table, he invited the whole family to dinner and announced the main meal would be the large turtle we had caught. Mother said she would stay home; she was not up to eating turtle. But Uncle Cal was a prankster and told her he would make a special chicken dish just for her. Then he swore me to secrecy, saying a large turtle had seven different kinds of meat a good chef could identify and he could make part of the meat look like chicken, smell like chicken and taste like chicken. Mother happily ate the "chicken" and declared forever after that she would never eat turtle. On my honor, I never said a word to anyone.

A mile and a half up the mountain road is Orion Hines' farm, which borders on the farm where my father was born. Orion owns 1,000 acres of the mountaintop but his farm was on the road itself and he had a farm stand in front of his house. My father's farm was maybe 400 yards from the road, and he and Orion became close friends. The Hines' family was the link between the past and present in my father's life.

Orion was the recognized, skilled hunter and trapper in the area. Fur coats were popular at the time and fox and raccoon pelts brought good prices. Dad and Orion hunted together and this kept them close over the years. Dad owned his World War 1 rifle. He also had a 54-gauge shotgun for hunting wild turkeys, a 30-30-gauge rifle with a telescope for deer hunting and a 22-gauge for hunting squirrels. (Mother was as good as they get in preparing wild meat for the dinner table.)

Orion had several dogs that were trained to hunt raccoons. At one time, Dad paid $75 for a trained coonhound, which he called "Old Lead" because he usually led the pack when they were out hunting. I loved to go with them at night following the baying of the hounds. My job was to carry the carbide lamps. Climbing steep mountainsides at night is an experience you never forget.

Even in the old days, the Hines were old-fashioned. Mrs. Hines' parents didn't like "store boughten" socks so her mother spun the wool to knit wool socks, and Orion became the best sheep shearer in the area. Orion's wife Lew baked bread and they sliced it an inch thick, then slathered it with homemade butter or honey. Honey was important to them and it was never store boughten.

In the fall they set out a dish of honey to draw honeybees. A war ensued between the competing wild bees, and the strongest would carry off the honey. Then the bee line (they travel in a straight line) would reveal the location of the hive, usually in the hollow limb of an old tree. A large hive might yield several hundred pounds of honey. Dad loved to participate in all this. He had escaped subsistence farming through getting an education but he still loved certain aspects of farming. Dad and Orion raised domestic bees together, and I helped clean the wooden pound boxes of excess wax in preparing the honey for sale. Dad got 25 cents a pound for his honey, most of which he sold to the owner of the Natwick Lumber Company.

Lew was tiny and weighed about 85 pounds, but she was a dynamo of energy. The primary gardener, she grew vegetables and fruit, then put up several hundred cans of food for the winter. Her mother and father lived with them and grandmother was also tiny. She had lost most of her teeth early in life and she had a long pointed chin, which caused me to stare. I often wondered how long it would take before her chin touched her nose when she chewed.

Across the road from the ancient farmhouse was an apple and peach orchard. The peach trees produced an old-fashioned fruit, about half the size of the fruit produced by scientifically improved trees. My father prized the old-fashioned fruit.

Orion and Lew had a son and daughter. Their son built a house on land he inherited from his father and was then on his own, but Ruth was the pride of the family and my father was especially fond of her, partly because he had no daughter of his own. She was a good student and rode the school bus to the high school in Moorefield, but tragedy struck the family. In her younger years, she developed a rare disease that got worse as she grew older and eventually crippled her. This devastated my father almost as much as her family. She was taken to the best clinic but they could do nothing. The last time I visited her with my father, she was lying on a cot, her spine twisted grotesquely, her muscles in spasm as she heroically tried to type her school lessons. She died at 21.

Chapter 4

Church

The church has always played a big part in my life, especially Duffy Memorial Methodist in Moorefield. It was another source of community for these isolated farmers and a fine place for us kids to get some religion and socialize too. I met the wonderful Park family and became close to them. They had two boys and we had three, so we naturally gravitated into one big family.

Our parents liked to play "set back" at our house, a card game, and "caroms", a game that used a wooden playing board with corners like a pool table. Anyway, the object of the game was to shoot wooden rings into the holes with a flip of your finger. While they played downstairs we boys got into pillow fights upstairs. We always had lots of fun and then the worst thing imaginable happened and everything changed.

Ralph Park was diagnosed with Bright's disease. The fact of his illness sobered our activities and nothing was quite so much fun anymore. Once again, it was Father who sought treatment. Ralph died that very same year, at 14, and was buried in the cemetery at Asbury church. We often visited his grave and I felt real sorrow over this in a way I had not felt before.

Gladys Park eventually married Brian Lambert. He and Father formed a partnership to raise chinchillas for profit, which never did quite pan out because their sale was controlled by an association. But Mother had several chinchilla wraps, acquired just before the fad was over and the coats went out of style.

The Duffy Memorial Methodist Church, where I was baptized just two doors away from my house, had a strong voice in the community.

People listened to the opinions of Duffy's pastor and those opinions carried weight. When the Reverend Raymond Musser became pastor of the church, he had great influence on me. Both he and his wife Louise loved music. Louise had a trained operatic voice, the very opposite of the country music so in vogue today. With their arrival, a youth choir started up. I was in it—boys could sing without being considered feminine, and I have sung in choruses ever since. Rev. Musser was the one who "made music in Moorefield." At one youth rally, he managed to gather nearly 900 young people from surrounding towns to sing, a small miracle for a small town in West Virginia.

I went to Sunday school, which was taught by elected lay teachers who used a Methodist curriculum, and I also went to Wednesday night prayer meetings. Every summer my brothers and I went to a church camp, one in Manassas, Virginia and another in West Virginia. In Manassas, I was beginning to gain some self-confidence (it was the first year I was free of bed wetting.) The most popular study group was called Boy-Girl relationships, and I was ripe for this. I liked a girl from Virginia and we spent lots of time together, but our friendship came to an abrupt end and I never had a chance to say goodbye.

The day before we were due back home, a member of my neighborhood gang, Huck Seymour, challenged us to a pancake-eating contest. I lost after eating 18 of the things. Huck won with 19. The next morning as we were packing, I felt ill. I thought it was the pancakes but two lumps sprouted in back of my ears and I had a severe headache. The doctor diagnosed me with the mumps, which were very contagious. I rode home with a camp counselor and felt half dead when they carried me into the house. Charles and Rodney slipped out the back door as I was brought in. Strangely, no one at camp or home contracted the mumps.

Believe it or not, one hundred men attended the "One Hundred Men's Bible Class." It was a perfect group for Father because he had some problems with regular Sunday church—he didn't like organ music or soprano voices. He took to this study group, however, and served as attendance secretary. Four teachers taught the men and it was an honor to be elected to teach. During the sessions, the old farmers would fall asleep and snore—I guess they were forgiven because nobody made a fuss about it. A separate women's group was active too, numbering about 30 or 40 women. In high school, the kids had Bible study as well.

The church was the center of most of our social life outside the extended family. In those days the bishop appointed the minister, usually for two years. If he was very popular, he might be appointed for an extra year. Reverend Musser was at Duffy for three years, then transferred to a plot of land with a handful of people in Virginia and asked to build a church. Meanwhile, it was my luck that I came of age during the Musser years. The couple welcomed me into their home and lives and, under their influence, I decided to become a minister.

I remember listening to a lively debate in the men's class about what makes a pastor great. So many different answers! Some thought preaching was the most important thing, and Rev. Lambert was best at that. No one ever forgot his Shakespeare sermon. He would stand on the front porch of the post office and greet everyone who came in, then disappear until the Sunday sermon. The men remembered Rev. McDonald and his outstanding family of five children; they remembered another who raised enough money to get the church out of debt, and another who was a very good administrator. But I will always remember Rev. Musser and his wife for their leadership of youth in music. Five young men decided to become Methodist ministers under their leadership.

Rev. Musser felt that movies were a big influence on adults and kids so he was careful about what his children saw. His son Jay was five when his father decided to take him to a Western.

"There are good cowboys and bad ones," his father told him. "You can choose to be a good one but don't be a bad one." The movie was not what Rev. Musser expected, and Jay took the lesson to heart. The next day he broke two windows in the basement of the parsonage shooting at his sister, which is exactly what the good cowboys had done in the movie the night before. After this, Rev. Musser talked a lot about "developing sound judgment."

Church was great fun for me and gave me a liberal philosophy to believe in. The leaders against slavery in the Valley were Quakers and their ideas influenced the Methodists, which then touched us. Yes, the church instilled a sense of guilt and original sin. You had to be saved or you were doomed to hell. But we were kids and could live with this. We would formulate our own ideas later.

School

I notice I haven't said very much about school, and I'm not sure why. Our grade school was a one-room schoolhouse and it's funny what you remember. I remember that we had a rotund teacher, a lady whose brother had cancer and his face was half-eaten away. It was a horrible thing for me to see, but I'm sure it was worse for him. He didn't live long. On the whole, I find that I have certain images of school rather than day-to-day recollections.

Here is another image I haven't forgotten. Our grade school building served as the home of many mice. During class, I often watched them play and search for food in the debris in a wall grating. The mice must have followed me all the way to high school because there they were again. When we entered the building at night for various rehearsals, the minute we turned on the lights, we could see mice scattering in every direction. The year after I graduated, a new consolidated high school was built to serve three previous schools, and my old high school building was renovated and became the new elementary school. I assume the mice went along with the plan and were not disturbed.

In another of those images, I remember that Susan Welton and I were sent to the back of the room in grade school because we already knew our numbers and the alphabet and we had nothing to learn. Our education had been going on all along at home; others were not so lucky. But there was another reason we were advanced too. We were always the oldest kids in the class as our birthdays were a few days after the cut-off date, which gave us a clear advantage.

I remember the graduation ceremony at the end of eighth grade, which was held in the McCoy Theater. I had to give a speech and I memorized it right down to the last word. Then in the middle of my speech, my mind went blank. I had it written down on a paper in my pocket, but it seemed like it was miles away. Mother and her best friend, Mrs. Friddle, were sitting in the front row and they motioned to me to retrieve it and carry on. With great dignity, I thought, I casually reached in my pocket, pulled out the paper, found my place and resumed speaking. What happened? The audience applauded. That triumphant moment was the beginning of my growing confidence. I realized I could make mistakes in front of friends and family and live through it—I did not have to be afraid. I was applauded for my recovery and that felt good. A big lesson learned young.

Chester Hiett was the Vo-Ag teacher in Moorefield High School and was also Father's close friend. He was a practical joker but serious too. Among other things, he had developed the community cannery, which greatly benefited the farmers. The day he got married was a special day for the entire town. The community celebrated by presenting the couple with gifts and congratulations, but they also recognized an opportunity when they saw one. It was payback time for the many tricks Chester had played on numerous people. What better time than the day of his wedding?

After the ceremony, Chester happily left the church with his bride, anticipating his honeymoon with relish and, lo and behold, he found all four wheels missing from his car. Surely he had a friend in the crowd who would help him. He asked this person, then that person to loan him a car. They all refused even though he was a town superstar. There would be no honeymoon. But as I said, it was payback time and paybacks can go both ways.

At dusk, a large hay wagon hooked to a team of horses arrived at his house loaded with friends with noisemakers—trumpets, drums, sleigh bells, cymbals, pipes and, best of all, a saw blade from the mill that measured three feet across. With a din loud enough to wake the dead, the wagon made its way over every street in town. At this point, Chester expected to get his car back and he was relieved that he and his bride had endured. But, no. Now it was time to share memories of past events. So Chester and his bride were the center of raucous attention while everyone shared a story or two with the crowd. It was a scene out of "This is Your Life." Mother remembered the lima bean in the can of water. Someone else remembered the "fizzeron" in the coffee cup. There were so many memories, the crowd said they needed a second night of "belling and telling." And so it went.

Eventually Chester and his lady made their get-away.

An incident occurred when I was in high school that has haunted me to this day. When we moved back to town from the mill, we lived on the south end of Elm Street next to the jail. I spent a lot of time with Uncle Robert who was just four years older and more like a peer. We spent many an evening shooting at English sparrows in the ivy on the jail wall with our BB guns. Uncle Robert was my fishing partner too.

One day we were fishing at Augdon Hole, a deep pond in the main river below Moorefield. A man who had been harvesting asked us to take him across the river in an old derelict rowboat that was wasting away on the beach. We had thought of using the boat ourselves but saw that it was not seaworthy. When we said "no," the man decided to go by himself and defiantly took the boat out. Paddling away, he made it half way across the pond when the boat abruptly went over and he went with it. No doubt it was taking on water from the outset and he hoped he would make it across the river before things became serious. The man had heavy boots on and could not save himself. He began to yell for help. Robert was a strong swimmer and he promptly jumped in and swam, reaching the man before I could, but it was no use. The man drowned. Robert was given accolades for his attempt to save him.

Bad Boys

Moorefield had its share of toughs and one was Jackie Stover whose father owned a store downtown. Jackie helped himself to anything he wanted, even though his father got angry when he stole for his gang. He seldom wore clean clothes, often needed a bath and was pretty much a street urchin. All his parents' attention went to their daughter who was beautiful, well dressed and had one of the most expensive fur coats in town. The spoiling of the daughter and the neglect of the son were the talk of the town. No one ever knew why they favored the girl over the boy.

Jackie Stover had a hideaway near the Duffy Memorial Methodist Church, an old icehouse that could only be entered from the top. He called it his fort. He was the leader of a small gang of boys who were aggressive and territorial. Our neighborhoods touched but my friends and I made an effort to stay clear of them. One day my brother Charles got into a fight with Jackie and ended up with a bruised lip that was so swollen it needed medical attention. Jackie praised his fine work, taunting Charles and saying he was a jerk because his lip "hung way down." Jackie was a rowdy kid and the town was always full of his voice.

Our group was more interested in hunting and fishing, exploring the woods and fields, often with BB guns in tow, which were legal and popular. The conflict between the two groups grew increasingly tense and the outcome could have been serious. When BB guns began looking more like weapons of war than playthings, my father and others were alarmed enough to get the BB guns taken off the street.

As an avid reader, I was already interested in understanding how gangs formed and how nicknames came about. My nickname was Soup Bean. My best friend was Scotty Reynolds, who was a mere hundred pounds and had a high squeaky voice. At 17, he shot up like a cornstalk and stood six feet tall. When a tuft of hair appeared on his Adam's apple, his nickname changed from "half pint" to "turkey." A third member, "Huck", was the biggest of the gang, with a nickname that came from the huckleberry pie that frequently appeared in his lunch box. "Satchel" was the fourth member.

One day Jackie fell from the top of his icehouse den and broke his hip, which put him in the hospital. His loud, piercing voice was not heard for over 24 hours. The community had no expectations for Jackie, even in small matters like making it home at suppertime—he was on his own schedule. Unfortunately, he developed TB of the bone and became crippled. My brother Charles visited him in a treatment center. When Charles later died in the China Typhoon, Jackie cried and said he was the only person who had ever cared about him.

Our neck of the woods came to be famous for something much more notorious than Jackie Stover's gang. Our region spawned the Shoemaker gang, a small group of hoodlums and gangsters who made headline news for nearly three years. Their specialty was terrorizing local citizens in Moorefield and neighboring towns, while state and local police hunted them down in the wild mountainous regions of West Virginia, Maryland and Virginia. Little did I know I would come quite so close to the action. In the middle of the night, I was awakened by gunfire. I jumped up out of bed. What in God's name was happening? It turned out that three members of the notorious Shoemaker gang had been cornered and captured almost outside my window—two were now in custody and a third was dead.

The episode ended up on the national radio program, "Gangbusters," and I felt very close to the drama. Sergeant Shields of the state police had been renting the other side of our double house and he was one of the leading characters. An excellent woodsman, he had traced the gang's activities and located their hiding places in some of the numerous caves in the area. The gang had a favorite target, gun stores, as they were obviously building up an arsenal. A friend of the family, Raymond Orndorf, had opened a gun store in an old farm on Simon Bean Mountain and the Shoemakers robbed the store three different times.

The saga of the Shoemaker gang actually began some years back when they and their cousins, the Futz boys, came to Moorefield on Saturdays to shop and sell their produce. Two of the Shoemakers and one of the Futzes had served time in jail so the town was wary and kept an eye out. The Shoemakers were a rowdy bunch and often got drunk, which led to trouble with the local policeman, Mr. Robinette. They would stride into the Busy Bee, a popular gathering place with a luncheonette and pool hall, as if they owned it.

On this crazy day, a younger Shoemaker boy was drunk and began arguing with the policeman, Mr. Robinette. He grabbed the top off one of the stools where the customers sat and smashed the officer in the head, injuring him. The war had begun.

Well, Mr. Robinette was walking home one evening when he heard two men talking about robbing a store. He needed to make a plan and get some help to thwart the robbery. He called a gun-owner, Mr. Powell, and deputized him and another citizen, giving them instructions to comb the town and see what they could see. The three found nothing suspicious and retired to the Busy Bee. Suddenly they saw a flash of light coming from the dry goods store next door.

Mr. Robinette moved fast, heading out and moving quietly to the back of the dry goods store as the thieves were moving toward the front door, carrying feed sacks full of goods. He called out to the men—"Stop right where you are." One of the men looked back and fired, hitting the officer in the thigh and breaking his thighbone. As he went down, the policeman fired back and killed one of the Shoemaker brothers. The other brother ran full speed out of the store, shattering the front door in his flight. He was arrested the next day hiding under his grandmother's bed. Now that was one cowardly way to go! The arrest warrant, of course, sent the rest of the family back to the woods, but this event was just the beginning of their story.

The gang vowed vengeance on Officer Robinette, and our small Appalachian towns suffered from their brutality. As their raids on the mountain farmers increased, everyone became more terrified. But if citizens turned in information on their whereabouts, they would be visited in the night, threatened, and their cows, pigs and horses would be shot. The raids on gun stores continued and then they found a new source of weapons. When deer hunters returned to their locked cars where they had stored their guns, they found their cars shot full of holes and the guns gone.

Eventually the state stationed an army of lawmen in Moorefield in an effort to put an end to the Shoemaker gang. A plan was made and a rumor flew about town that a payroll of $100,000 dollars was in the safe at the Farm Bureau. Word had reached the lawmen that the Shoemakers were not surviving well in the mountains and were without money and food. The lawmen expected they would raid the Farm Bureau and they waited nearly a week.

Finally, three men showed up in the dead of night. The oldest son broke into the office where the safe was kept. Little did he know that Mr. Shields was hiding in the office. "Drop your gun," he shouted. The robber wasted no time and tried to gun him down but it was pitch dark and his bullet hit the refrigerator. He then dove through the front window and was greeted by a hail of bullets. The cops said he was dead before he hit the ground. The second son surrendered in the warehouse. The third son stuck a sawed-off shotgun in the stomach of a policeman, but it didn't fire and this Shoemaker boy was captured. He was 17. Apparently the gang had run low on shells or their gunpowder was wet.

A sociological study was done of the families involved in these events and their backgrounds were predictable: The families were poor, uneducated and had a history of violence. They came from a region where making illegal moonshine was a major source of income. Being outside the law was the norm for the family. When one of the five sons told his father he was hungry, his father gave him a gunnysack and said, "Go find something." Indeed they did. They went to the nearest mountain farm and raided the storage room of canned goods and hams.

When gunshots woke me up in the night so long ago, I believed I was hearing the last hurrah of the Shoemaker boys. And I was.

Camp Seldom Seen

Camp Seldom Seen became the source of many happy, wild memories during my high school years, and it acquired that name for good reason—it was remote as remote could be. Go south of Wardensville on Lost River to the edge of George Washington National Forest and you will find the small town of Largent. Here your journey begins in search of the camp in the deep, deep wilderness owned by Chester Hiett, the vocational agricultural teacher in Moorefield. The only way to reach it is by trudging along an ancient logging road for six miles and, at times, we had to literally create the road as we went along. There were ditches to be covered, stones to be broken with a sledgehammer, logs to be cut. At the end of the road was a big log cabin built into the side of the mountain. This little piece of heaven looked down on a cold, strong, spring of water. A unique second story opened into the yard. The first floor kitchen opened onto a patio bordered by a stone wall.

At the time, the log cabin had not been used for years but one day in midsummer Chester decided to make it useful. He, along with Scotty Reynolds, Wendell Welton, my father and I hiked up the road loaded with camping supplies for a week's stay. The log roads were originally made by large trucks that plodded through the virgin forest; the loggers made repairs with axes, spades, crosscut saws and sledgehammers. By now, the old roads had nearly disappeared and we took most of the day to reach the camp, using our own tools to keep the road passable.

My excitement was high as I knew the river was chock full of black bass, sunfish and goggle eyes. As soon as we arrived, I took my fishing pole and headed for the river, quickly catching a very respectable bass. Then srrrrrrrrrr—I heard a commotion in the weeds and froze when I saw a large copperhead snake three feet away. I ran back to camp and told my story to the men. They listened but were not too impressed. Then we were in the kitchen when Chester noticed a copperhead lying on the stone wall ten feet away. He ran for his 22 rifle and shot it—now the situation was serious. Mr. Hiett declared war on the snakes, saying we would have to destroy them to make the camp safe.

That night as it got dark, we lit a fire in the fireplace and gathered around it, partly for protection. After all, how many snakes might be in the cabin? No one said this but we were thinking it. The next morning we killed several more snakes by the rock wall, then headed for the river. The copperheads had taken refuge in holes along the slate bank of the river, which had partly dried up. With poles and fishing gear we snagged them out of their holes and killed 36 snakes in three days.

Chester Hiett was his usual sunny self, always poking fun and teaching lessons. When we were hunting the snakes, I bragged that I had never gotten close to a snake because I would see it before it moved. My x-ray eyes could spot those slithery, slippery bodies yards away and I could finish them off from a distance without poking into their business. That was enough for Chester. So one evening we were trudging through an open field along the river and came to bare ground. I thought it strange that the men gave me the carbide light and made me lead the column—with my father right behind me.

Then, ohmigod, whoa. There in front of me was an enormous rattlesnake and my foot was about to come down, splat, on his belly or back. I jumped a good foot in the air, nearly knocking my father down. But when I looked again to gauge the snake's revenge, I could see that he wasn't moving. He was dead as a doornail and slowly I realized this was Chester's revenge. What a big klutzy fool I was. Chester took great delight in showing me my heel mark where I had almost stepped on the corpse. Dead or alive, I hadn't seen this snake at all. Bragging gets you nowhere—this was his lesson.

On another trip to Camp Seldom Seen, we traveled the arduous road, then discovered that someone had broken into the camp and taken all the utensils, leaving us nothing to cook with. Chester asked us to take out our pocketknives and he led us in the direction of a nearby dried out, very dead apple tree. Oh, of course. We cut into the tree and crafted our own utensils—knives, forks, spoons and several wooden bowls. His latest lesson was that we could handle primitive conditions and still enjoy a good meal. When other friends joined us later, we simply carved more utensils and it became a sort of survival lesson.

The biggest thrill was fishing in these waters. For larger bass, we fished with catfish minnows as bait, keeping them alive in the spring water. Here they were literally immobilized by the cold water, even the active catfish. My father not only loved to fish but he was willing to clean them as well. He spent most of his time cleaning the dozens of fish we had the pleasure of catching. Over the years, different people came to Camp Seldom Seen, including teachers from the high school. Meals were great, sometimes prepared by my teachers but most of the time by Mr. Dispenet, the superintendent who filled our plates with fish and wild game—turkey, ducks and pheasants.

High School

There were 37 kids in my class at Moorefield High School, which was actually a large number for our area. I lived in town so it was easy for me to get there, but some of the students lived 20 miles from the school and they traveled by bus over steep, not-too-dependable roads. Here and there ditches were dug to keep rainwater from washing out the road—we called them "thank you mams." Often the bus driver had to shift gears to lessen the jolt. I graduated with two girls who traveled the farthest and never missed a day of school.

The schools had been consolidated and a new building was opening next year. This new spirit of cooperation brought out the best in people. Moorefield was also performing well in sports and the year after I graduated, we became the state champions in football and basketball. A new sense of equality grew between adults and children, teachers and students.

I didn't dance and couldn't play basketball but I excelled as a student and was a happy kid with my buddies who fished and hunted. Both my brothers were star athletes. As I said, Charles grew to be six feet three inches. He was a fast runner and his scoring record was among the best in both football and basketball. Rodney was a big guy too, six feet one, and equally good but at times he took risks with the ball that angered his coach. On one occasion, he intercepted the ball in the end zone and ran it for 104 yards. Had he fumbled, the other team would have won, thus ruining a perfect season. He played basketball too.

Eventually I grew to be six feet tall too and Father was amazed at his three tall sons, considering that he was on the small side—five feet seven and 135 pounds. He said he would have to grow a mustache to help the townspeople know who was father and who was son.

I had girls who were friends but no girlfriends. One group was called the Crazy Seven and they did whacky things to entertain us—I think that's what they were doing. One swallowed a fishing worm in class and another gave the principal a piece of Exlax, passing it off as candy. Tame stuff by today's standards but it was over-the-top behavior then. On Cape Cod years later, I met a woman from that group, now the dignified wife of a Falmouth lawyer who was mortified to be reminded of some of her high school antics.

My biggest grief was my teeth. I always suffered with decaying teeth and had broken off a part of two front teeth, so I looked pretty awful. My general health wasn't the best. I had low resistance to infections and easily picked up childhood illnesses. My dental care was limited because my father simply couldn't afford it.

Though I wasn't good at sports, I often went along on trips as the teams needed warm bodies. In one town we played basketball in a building with such low ceilings, you could not take a long shot. A red pot-bellied stove heated the room and this stove sat stolidly in our way, coming at us like a sixth man on their team—we would not get close to it. We never won in that room.

My senior year we traveled to Grafton, West Virginia to play in the state tournament and were defeated in the first round. Hence, we were free from the training rules and had some time on our hands. It was bitterly cold and our rooms were without heat. We spent what money we had in town, buying a bunch of cigars, returning to our freezing rooms and lighting up. Soon the air was thick with cigar smoke and we felt nauseous. We struggled to open the heavy storm windows and could not budge them. I was ferociously sick; I cannot remember ever being so sick. This one event was the biggest influence on my decision not to smoke, outweighing all the high-powered advertisements that try to persuade us.

My father was a veteran, which made me eligible from the Moorefield district to attend a summer program at the Marston Mill. The purpose was to teach young people how to organize a state government like the one in West Virginia. I don't even remember which party I was assigned to because something bigger happened. On the grounds, a flowerbed had been built around a huge stone used to grind wheat and other grains into flour. It had been set in concrete to keep it standing up. A little five-year-old boy was climbing up on top and sliding down the other side. He pulled the stone and it fell on his knee crushing it. His screams of pain brought a crowd. I ran over to help. Two of us boys used all our muscle power to lift the stone and free the child. I remember feeling good that I was there to help. That incident helped shape my desire to help when there was trouble, and not shrink from it.

One of the attractions of Marston Mill was George Laudenslaugher, the most famous chef in West Virginia. I asked him if I could have the recipe for his legendary bread, which he gave me and I have used to this day. Even with his recipe, I have never been able to make bread as tasty as my mother's rolls. There were no exact directions in his measurements, just a handful of flour and so forth, which just wasn't good enough.

On the whole, I had fun and felt free in high school and could even get away with leaving classes early with Scotty Reynolds in order to go fishing. The principal said later that I more than made up for it as I always finished my work before departing and Scotty was becoming a more responsible student as a result of his relationship with me. Besides, you might say there was a more important education taking place at the fishing hole than in class. I graduated from Moorefield High School in 1940 at the head of my class. I was the only one went on to college. Many of my fellow graduates became chicken farmers.

Chapter 5

Western Maryland College

The pastor of Duffy Memorial Church in Moorefield had accomplished something close to a miracle. Over the years, Reverend Musser actually got five of us boys to declare for the Methodist ministry. He informed my family that Western Maryland College had been created to provide education for Methodist ministers and the scholarship offered to theological students, $350 would pay half the cost. It was good money in those days. By its charter a majority of the board of trustees at WMC were Methodists and the college president was required to be a Methodist as well.

I had also been accepted at Wesleyan College in West Virginia but the scholarship to Western Maryland tipped the scales, and I arrived on campus as the only student from my state. WMC was in Westminster, thirty miles west of Baltimore, and surrounded by rolling hills and rich farmland. It had a natural amphitheater for a football field and a nine-hole golf course—it was an elitist school and not many blacks were seen on campus. There were only ten black students in a student body of 800.

I was assigned a room with the football players and my roommate, Arlie Mansberger, was the son of a Methodist minister from Pennsylvania. He was the quarterback for the football team and was on an athletic scholarship. The school has an interesting history with regard to scholars and athletes. Football had been a big time activity at WMC under a famed coach, Dick Harlo, who had won a national championship. But the college also prided itself on its academic reputation and especially its status in having one of the best pre-med programs in the country. That image suffered somewhat as football began to dominate a school founded to train Methodist ministers.

Interestingly, the trustees rebelled and came out with new rules that said that athletic scholarships could only be awarded to football and basketball players who were scholars first and athletes second. Imagine this happening today! So I was a beneficiary too, being thrown in with football players who were serious students. And right here I'll say that Arlie Mansberger was by far the most intelligent of them all.

My high school hadn't really prepared me for a rigorous academic life. It prepared us to be good chicken farmers. Our teachers were leaders in developing information and techniques in raising chickens for a growing market in the nearby cities. In truth, I had always thought of joining my father in the insurance business, and it was my minister, Rev. Musser, who gave me big ideas. Arlie came from a different world. He was already a serious student and planned to be a doctor. We studied together every day and he seemed not to mind that it took me longer to learn new material. Arlie was amazing in so many ways—this top scholar played the trombone and led pep rallies before the football games.

Arlie was a good influence and a great friend. He was also a tease and soon I was known all over campus as a "Hoopie," or a hick, a new name for someone from West Virginia. I had heard West Virginians called plain ole hicks, ridge runners, snake eaters and hillbillies, but this was a new one. His sister, a senior at WMC, and even his father joined in on the fun, but the last laugh was on them. Arlie was astonished when his father sent him a telegram telling him the family would be moving to Wheeling, West Virginia. As a Methodist minister, he had to go where the church sent him. So Arlie's father learned of his new assignment at the recent Annual Methodist Conference. Now there were two of us Hoopies! This cemented our friendship.

Alcohol was taboo on this Methodist campus, or any Methodist campus, for that matter. Students could drink in town but would be expelled if they got drunk. Nevertheless, drinking was rampant. Arlie and I did not drink at all, the only students in the athletes' dorm who could say this. The message I heard while growing up in the Methodist church was that alcohol was a dangerous substance and we should treat it like we would a West Virginia rattlesnake. My parents reinforced this teaching by their actions.

At first our fellow students did not accept our sobriety and kept trying to get us to join them. We actually did but managed not to drink. It took six months for them to realize we really weren't going to indulge and after that the tables turned. We would have lost status had we become drinkers. We played a role—we drove the cars, separated the combatants and got people home safely. And we never lectured! So they must have appreciated us. If I had a dollar for every student I helped up the hill and into the dorm, I would be swimming in bills.

Arlie was the only student in a class of 17 who earned an A in the pre-med program's toughest course. As a quarterback he was fast but, for some reason, he was always injuring himself. He separated his shoulder, sustained a severely sprained ankle, had a concussion that caused blackouts for a week and, finally, in his third year he broke his leg. His father disliked football and didn't wish his son to play. In fact, Arlie was playing football without his father's knowledge. I was sworn to secrecy about his playing and so was his sister. The broken leg was serious and medical care for athletes was not the best so I became his nurse. After he experienced six days of agony, I called his father.

I came to believe that Arlie had brittle bones. He was quick, strong and willing to sacrifice his body for the sake of his team but his constant injuries suggested that something wasn't right. When one of the guards made a move that ended up separating his shoulder, he was taken out, his shoulder was taped up and he was put back in game. The same thing happened again in the next game. It happened so often during the season that when he joined the boxing team he could throw his shoulder out with a simple punch.

Arlie was a near-perfect roommate except that he had difficulty distinguishing between what was his and what was mine. If we each had dates and I had one shirt and he had none, he would take my shirt and leave if I wasn't there to grab it.

In psychology class, we were learning about hypnosis and after class we experimented on our own. In the lounge we discussed whether a person would act against his own wellbeing while under hypnosis. A coed agreed to be hypnotized and we told her how hot the room was getting. Sweat began to show on her brow. Then we told her how cold the room was and she shivered. But boys will be boys. When we told her to take off her clothes, she broke out of the trance and was angry. We concluded a person would not compromise her own best interest while under hypnosis.

But maybe, maybe they would do something silly, I mused, seeing my chance to get back at Arlie. Later that night, he was getting ready for a date, dressed in a dark suit and quite dapper. He was in a jovial mood and had some time to kill so I talked him into being put under.

I instructed him carefully and firmly. "When you wake up, your head will itch and only talcum powder can stop it."

He woke up and started shaking a blizzard of powder all over his hair and navy suit. He looked like the flour doughboy.

"That's for taking my last shirt," I grinned.

No matter what, we always remained friends. He later became a doctor and surgeon at Duke University.

Because Arlie was so popular, our room became a social center. I never went to bed before 2 a.m. and ended up losing 22 pounds my first year.

Social Life

The social life of the college was dominated by an ROTC unit. It was compulsory the first two years and all physical activity was directed through it. If you got through that, you could advance to become a second lieutenant in the army. Dances were organized military affairs. Dance cards were required in which you recorded the requests for your partner—it was our responsibility to see that our partner danced with many others. I had never learned to dance, partly because of my lack of coordination and partly for cultural reasons. Several coeds tried to teach me but I was hopeless and ended up just twirling my partners.

There were four fraternities, all locals, on campus and I joined one. When I was initiated during hell week, I had to carry a concert bass drum around wherever I went. Wild stuff. The big thing in my fraternity was playing pinochle.

Chapel was compulsory on Sunday nights and attendance was taken. Peck Bond, a friend, monitored attendance and then left the building. We debated religious issues endlessly. He was proud of the fact that he had attended only one religious event in his life, had never read the Bible but nevertheless had an opinion on everything religious.

He had a lovely sister who wanted to come to the graduation ball. Would I invite her as my date? I agreed on one condition—he would have to attend the full session of chapel that evening. He said he would but complained that his perfect record of never attending a chapel service in his four years was now broken. Because of me.

I can't remember the date very well but I do remember dating a girl from my roommate's hometown. She had never had a serious drink before and earlier in the day she brought a bottle of gin onto campus, which was against the rules. I'm sure she had help drinking it, but she finished it off herself and was still drunk when we went out that evening. I hadn't been briefed and didn't know what was wrong with her. All I remember is we did a lot of rolling around in a huge pile of leaves. The next day I expressed surprise that she had been drunk, much to the amusement of all my friends.

I met another friend, Milton Huber, who also wanted to become a Methodist minister. Tall, handsome, brilliant, he would become a lifelong friend. He was involved in one of those love stories one never forgets. Both he and his roommate met a young woman named Ruth at the same time and both wanted to date her. Milton graciously backed off and let his roommate do the courting. For three years, the two—Ruth and Milt's roommate—had one of the few permanent relationships on campus.

When his ROTC unit was called for duty, it was a sad parting. He was sent to England and not long after, he stopped writing. To her astonishment, she learned that he had met and married a nurse. Ruth was devastated and went into a deep depression, losing a lot of weight. Doctors feared she might have a growth in the brain. Nothing helped and she continued to lose weight.

During this time, Milt was having a similar experience. He had started dating a beautiful girl who ended up in an auto accident. She was injured so severely that she could not have children. They were very much in love but she felt her condition would be a handicap to him as a minister. It became the subject of a long debate. Meanwhile, she began to see her old boyfriend while the debate was going on. Milt asked me to date her roommate just to see if I could find out what was going on. So I had several dates with a lovely, sexy blonde who was attending Emerson, a drama school, and I found out that Milt's girlfriend had decided to become engaged to her old boyfriend.

Six months later Milt learned about Ruth, looked her up and what happened was amazing. She was thrilled to see him, she got well and happy, they were married and raised four children. We stayed in touch over the years and while writing this paragraph, I got a call from Ruth who said Milt was dying of heart disease. They had a rich, full life together. Quite the story.

Academics

I had graduated from high school without a language, not knowing I would someday study for the ministry, so I had to take French my first year.

Our teacher, Mademoiselle Snader, was a strange bird. She was single and in love with every handsome man on campus. The rumor was that if you flirted a little with her, she would pass you. At the same time, she accused the football players of being residents of a country club and did not take their studies seriously—perhaps a legacy from the days at WMC when the football team won a national title. Her messages were certainly mixed.

But Arlie knew his football players had to be up to standard and he was an amazing leader. He organized study reviews in the dorm whenever we had exams. He and I translated the French lessons for the players and with Arlie's tutoring I passed French and so did the others.

I majored in sociology and psychology. Dr. James P. Earp was my principal teacher and on the day I graduated, he shook my hand and said, "You are the most uninitiated hillbilly I have ever met in my whole life."

Hillbilly? Well, okay. Uninitiated hillbilly? Maybe. But "most uninitiated hillbilly ever"? I had no idea how I felt about this.

Birds and Bees

Most of the ministry students spent Sunday evenings the first two years in the home of Professor Little where we had conversations about ethics and religion and the world and we could question everything. Those sessions taught me more than my classes and I determined to be a student of group dynamics. Another attraction in the Little home was their three beautiful daughters, and our disappointment was palpable when one of them married a professor.

One day I came out of a science lab and saw a swarm of bees on a limb high in an oak tree. I informed the science teacher and he asked me to watch where they landed while he went to get a hive. He said it should be in a bush close to the ground. At that moment, the swarm lit in a bush a distance away at the end of the campus. He asked me to give him a hand in capturing them.

"Where are your gloves and helmet?" I asked.

"You are not afraid of bees, are you?"

"No," I replied, "but my father always wore gloves and a helmet." The professor assured me they would not sting me. He knelt down and moved his hands slowly into the live mass of bees, so numerous they could fill a bushel basket. He found the queen, put her on the edge of the hive he had brought, and waited until most of them were in. At that moment, two of the guard bees started to fly close to my face and I took that as a sign to move on. I did not get stung but thought I wouldn't test his theory any further.

Work

As I said, my scholarship paid $350 but I needed another $350 to pay my way through. I took a job as the soda jerk in the campus refreshment stand, which wasn't bad because I got to know much of the student body. During the summer I had jobs making hay, teaching swimming at a YMCA camp, waiting tables. I was also a helper for a roofing company and carried bundles of shingles weighing 80 pounds up a 30-foot ladder, one after the other. At noontime, when we were eating our lunch one day, one of the crew said,

"So you came to take Jake's place?"

"Oh, I didn't know. What happened to Jake?"

"He got careless and had a little fall. Broke an arm, a leg and his back. He will not be returning. Trouble was, he talked too much, didn't pay attention, nailed one side of a support for a scaffolding and forgot to nail the other side."

I got the message—it's a dangerous job. Pay attention. One of our toughest assignments came at the end of summer when the temperature was in the 90s. We put a skylight on the roof of a building several stories high and had to carry all our equipment up the ladder to the first landing, then the second, then the third. We came down the same way. I made a decision right then and there I did not want to make my life's work a roofer.

I earned 75 cents an hour.

There were actually two Methodist churches at WMC, the Methodist Episcopal Church North and the Methodist Episcopal Church South and, not to confuse things, a third one was simply called the Methodist Church. These splits occurred as a result of the Civil War. At WMC, the two buildings of the North and South Episcopal Church were just feet apart. In 1954, a convening conference united the three branches into the Methodist church but they made one glaring mistake. The 400,000 black members were put into a separate organization called the central jurisdiction, which covered the entire United States. The compromise was supposed to settle the racial issue but it only made it worse.

The church may have made mistakes, but the Methodists truly believed in education. Even today, the church's mark is everywhere. I could not have gone to college without the financial help of the church. When I became director of Revival House in Fall River (more about this later), I noticed that the 'delinquent home for girls' next door was sponsored by the Methodists. Boston University itself was originally founded to educate Methodist ministers. The Methodists are wonderful social workers and they always take a stand on the side of what is just and right. They fought hard against the Jim Crow laws that kept blacks back. So I could never understand the "central jurisdiction" designation for blacks.

Chapter 6

Meeting Christine

When I came home that summer from college, I met a young woman named Christine McMillen and I've known her ever since. She had come to Moorefield to teach home economics in the high school. It turned out she didn't know a thing about cooking but she stood out like a shining light to the young men in the school. Blonde-haired and blue-eyed, five feet tall, she weighed a mere 85 pounds. My younger brother wrote her love poems and tried to date her, slyly asking her to chaperone a bowling party. She said she would and when he picked her up, he was alone.

"Where's the rest of the party?" she asked.

"This is it!" he said. Their date was over fast.

The next day the whole school teased her about it and the superintendent sternly reminded her that she was not supposed to date students. She was not pleased with my brother. Nevertheless, Rodney kept telling me I had to meet this teacher. The high school held the first dances the year Chris came to teach. Up to now, dancing had been considered immoral and not conducive to economic survival—you couldn't dance all night and plow the fields the next day. Dancing was seen as a waste of time and energy, but the school dances immediately gave more life to the school. Rodney loved to dance and so did Chris, but she was wary of him after their "date."

That summer I had a job shoveling "lime marl" to fertilize the hay fields. I had gone to the post office and saw Christine on her way out. She really caught my eye. I wanted to know her so I decided to ask her for a date and called seven times before I found her at home. She agreed to go for a walk with me and that is how our relationship began. We spent time together every day for the next six weeks. The local movie house showed a western every week and this was our entertainment. Or we walked or sat on benches and talked. When I returned to Western Maryland, we said we would write to each other, and we did. Our letters always bound us together.

Christine was from Morgantown, West Virginia, a place surrounded by coke ovens, and she had dreams of leaving Morgantown forever and becoming an artist—she wanted to create art more than anything in the world. At West Virginia University, she was forced to major in home economics because it was the only program in which she could study art. Very quickly I found myself falling in love with this vibrant teacher who had a glow about her—I thought she was beautiful and so did everyone else. She did not think she was attractive because her front teeth needed to be straightened.

We all had problems with our teeth, it seemed, and my problems were major. I had inherited soft teeth and had broken off part of my two front teeth and had no teeth whatsoever in my top jaw at the time. I ended up having all my teeth pulled—in the course of a week. The bleeding was profuse but the decision changed my life. I never weighed over 150 pounds until I had those teeth pulled. I must have been so busy fighting infections that I had no time to grow. So I had the dubious gift of false teeth at a young age. Charles also had soft teeth but was able to keep them through frequent dental visits. I lost mine through infection and injury.

I was intrigued about how a young woman like Christine, with her whole life ahead of her, could end up in Moorefield. I learned that she had two options after graduating from college. She had her teaching credentials and received two offers. She could teach on the Eastern Shore, which was twice as far from her home in Morgantown. Or she could go to Moorefield, a hundred miles from Morgantown. Schoolteachers were poorly paid and she could not afford a car. So she took the job closest to home, which was just my luck.

When I met her, she had just broken up with her fiancé, giving back her engagement ring. She'd had a simple change of heart and decided not to marry him. So she was foot-loose and fancy-free in a town with one movie theater, open on weekends, and a library, and of course church, as well as the summer part of her job, which was to supervise her students' chosen home projects. It may have seemed silly for a girl who lived in a university town with lots of activity to take a job in a rural cow town teaching farm girls Home Economics, but what choice did she have? She was very good at sewing and home management, but cooking was another story. She wasn't much interested in cooking as she had an older sister who took over when her mother was at work. Many of the girls knew more about cooking than she. She came armed with bulletins and printouts provided by the university, but no good cookbook. One of her jobs was to direct the senior girls in preparing one hot dish to add to the lunches brought from home, so armed with the pamphlet on recipes for school lunches, the girls started to make a large batch of brownies when one of them spoke up, "You can't make brownies without flour!" Sure enough, no flour was listed in the recipe. Without a cookbook or knowledge of how much would be required to add to the large amounts of everything else, what could they do? They served cocoa.

On weekends Chris took the bus back home, just to get out of there, but her contract ran for twelve months. She managed to rent a room for nine months from Mrs. Kuhn who owned a dry goods store. The last three months she stayed with the superintendent and his wife, my former English teacher.

Christine had one special friend, Louise Dix, a home demonstration agent who taught farm women efficiency and the use of modern gadgetry. She became a lifelong friend. Louise later married an agronomist; they went to Singapore as unofficial Methodist missionaries and developed a fast-growing rice for that country. Tragedy followed her. Her two sons caught polio and her husband died of polio. Her sons recovered and later "sponsored" her marriage to another agronomist at the University of Pennsylvania. Chris and Louise still communicate, some sixty years later.

I took some trips to Morgantown and got to know Chris's family. Her mother Edith had diabetes and had to give herself shots of insulin two or three times a day. She was an excellent seamstress, a very creative doll maker, and she worked in a clothing store.

Her father was a high school chemistry teacher and a soil tester in the summer. He kept complete results of his plantings year after year. Like my father, he had flat feet, but Mac also had painful bunions and shuffled when he walked. He was tied to a strict schedule so that neighbors said they could set their clocks when he left for school. In spite of his rigid habits, he had affection for his three daughters.

We would seem to have nothing in common—he was a rabid Republican and I was a Democrat—he hated President Roosevelt and I greatly admired him—but we liked each other. We had lots of laughs. And we talked baseball. Mac was a fierce fan of the Pittsburgh Pirates and this seeped into many a conversation.

After he died, we learned that he was so compulsive about saving that he had stashed money in stocks without the family knowing. His three daughters divided the $30,000, but they would much rather have had the money while they were growing up.

Both families approved the relationship between Chris and me, and my parents suspected I was thinking marriage. "Why do you want to marry a woman as skinny as that?" my mother asked. "You have to shake a sheet to find her."

After just one year in Moorefield, Chris moved to Cincinnati, having accepted a position in a junior high school, which included teaching art. She had two roommates and enjoyed her new place and new life. I took the train a couple of times to visit her there. On my first trip, a sailor and I sat on each end of my suitcase, as there was no room left in the car. I stayed in a downtown hotel and took the streetcar to Norwood where Chris lived. It was a hot summer and I remember hearing the crunch of cockroaches underfoot when I got off the bus.

On my second trip, my brother Rodney met me in the city and we took a taxi to her apartment. The driver asked if we wanted a joyride and before we could open our mouths, he took off, driving through downtown at 50 mph—I think he was nearly crazy with the heat and just wanted to keep the wind blowing through the car. Christine and I wrote to each other every day. But I must confess I went through a wild time before I made that final commitment.

The war years were a time of national turmoil, especially for young men who were subject to the draft. Nobody knew what the future would be, or whether there would be a future at all.

After Pearl Harbor was bombed, the campus went berserk. Every window in the dorm was broken that night, including mine, and I slept right through it. The men knew their college careers were over. I reported to my draft board but was turned down for military service because of my false teeth and an injured knee from an old skiing accident. So many men went in—I was one of 50 men left on campus with 800 women.

At this time an attractive young woman from Vermont named Jean Eddy transferred to WMC in the middle of the term. We were taking a course in Family and were asked to form couples to work out a family budget. Jean was on the other end of the row of seats and I leaned over and motioned—"You and I." And so we met and worked out a budget.

She told me about her boyfriend who was in the Air Force and stationed in Virginia; WMC was as close as she could get to him. We talked many times again while I was working at the soda bar and our relationship was close and comfortable. Her boyfriend was leaving for Texas to depart for the front.

One day Jean arrived with a question. "Tell me something. Why do you think he wants me to fly to Texas with his mother to say goodbye?"

"My best guess? To give you a ring," I replied, grinning.

A week later she flew to Texas and the next time she came to the soda bar, she took off one white glove, beamed from ear to ear, and showed me her glittery diamond. But within two weeks, her joy turned to sorrow. Her boyfriend had been killed on his first mission.

I spent a lot of time consoling her. I told Christine about Jean and said I was only offering sympathy, but I had to face facts. I was involved with two lovely women, Chris, a tower of strength, and Jean, who needed support. When Christine came to see me at WMC the next fall, it was a near disaster. I was so exhausted, I slept and was late picking her up at the train station. And though she was sure of her feelings for me, I felt I was suddenly and unexpectedly in love with two women and I didn't know how to sort it out.

Chris and I stopped writing every day. And I made a stupid decision. I stayed at school over Thanksgiving vacation, lying to Chris and saying I needed time to prepare for exams. Instead I went to see Jean who was at school too, serving as monitor of her dorm. On a cold evening, I arrived at the side entrance and she let me in. She was attracted to me, perhaps because I really was an uninitiated hillbilly. We went to her room and spent a lot of time talking but this night, and many more, ended with heavy petting.

At some point, I realized how completely I was betraying Christine. I had made a commitment to her and gone off track. I hoped she would take me back. Well, my wild time didn't last long. By Christmas of that year, I had lost both girlfriends.

Life goes on. I graduated from Western Maryland with majors in sociology and psychology at the end of that year, 1944, and was accepted at Boston University Theological School. My first apartment, owned by the university, was in Louisburg Square and so began my life in the city. I was now light years from the chicken farms of Moorefield. I was in Boston, pursuing my dream to become a Methodist minister.

Chapter 7

Boston University School of Theology

In those days, the theological school was located on Mount Vernon Street on Beacon Hill, near the State House. I arrived by bus about an hour before a hurricane decided to sideswipe the city and the wind was blowing and trees were down. I asked five different people how to find the school and I got five different answers, until finally I found it. I settled in my room in Louisburg Square, the heart of Boston, and was not reassured by fellow students who said, "The roof blew off this place during the 1938 hurricane."

My very first friendship was with Fay Gemmell and his wife, Charlotte, from Nebraska. They lived on the fourth floor of the Boy Scout building on Beacon Street and paid their rent by being caretakers of the place. Most of us had found jobs as waiters in local restaurants so we got a full meal and enough money to pay expenses.

Another close friend was Bill Keefe, who was from West Virginia. We often ate our meals in greasy spoon restaurants and twice came down with food poisoning. Bill and I decided to rent an apartment on Garden Street, the backside of Beacon Hill, as the rent was only $24 a month. A third roommate, Leonard, also from Nebraska, joined us. My roommates did not like each other and I often found myself in the middle as the referee.

The bigger war outside followed us here and then came home in a personal, devastating way.

The War

The year, 1944, was a time of turmoil and indecision for me. The war dominated our lives and young men everywhere were volunteering for the service. My brother Charles had been deferred because he was enrolled in a college in Tennessee to study dentistry. He felt it was his duty to enlist, so he left school and spent six weeks training in the Great Lakes Naval Training Center. He was assigned to the Spence, a new destroyer ready to go to sea. He ordinarily would not have been on this ship, but a vacancy occurred in the storehouse and Navy policy said the position had to be filled and Charles was it. The war was not going well. The Seventh Fleet to which he was assigned had retreated and his first action was in the battle of Kula Gulf.

Earlier that year, when I was still at Western Maryland, I was scheduled to give a piano recital. I wrote to him and asked him to be thinking about me at 4 p.m. the day of the recital—nothing scared me more than a piano recital. A month later I received a letter from him saying, "Brother, I was not thinking about you that afternoon." His ship had taken a hit from a Japanese shore battery and he had lost a buddy. Here I was playing the piano and he was getting shot at. After that I lost interest in piano lessons. My ROTC unit was called up this same year, 1944, and I would have gone as a second lieutenant in the infantry, but I could not pass the physical.

Charles was involved in fourteen major naval engagements, including the bombardment of the Japanese mainland, when his ship was lost in a fierce storm, typhoon Cobra. Three ships went down in the typhoon, taking close to 800 sailors with them to a watery grave. The ships were escorting the Third U. S. Fleet Fueling Group east of the Philippines, on their way to join up with Task Force 38 engaged in the invasion of Mindoro. They were bounced around in waves 70 feet high. Charles was one of 294 men who went down on The Spence; 23 survived. Later, in a first person account, a senior survivor noted that Charles had no doubt been below deck in his compartment. Later I made contact with a survivor who said he had been in the water 30 hours before being rescued.

Admiral William "Bull" Halsey was held responsible for failing to sail the Third Fleet ships out of the typhoon's path. The awful date was December 18, 1944.

For months, my brother Charles took over my mind. He was always there, not shadowy but real, and so was Moorefield and our days growing up. Charles was born in May, a gift of spring to our family. He was tall and handsome, a natural athlete. In his senior year, he was a key player in football when Moorefield won the state championship. My father did not want his sons to play football but Charles had said—"Father, you may as well get used to it. I am going to play football." And well he did. He was bright and cheerful. He couldn't carry a tune but sang the hymns in church with an exuberance that was contagious.

His closest friend was Kissi Bowman whose father was the best-known alcoholic in town. Charles was very protective of Kissi and once even beat him for getting drunk, telling him he would do it again if he had to. Kissi mourned the loss of his friend the rest of his life.

Charles and I had written to each other frequently and he had a code name for every island in the Pacific, so I always knew where he was located. He had come home on leave earlier when his ship was being repaired. It had taken a hit from a shore battery and his buddies had been killed and wounded. At that time, he said he was committed to finishing out this war but, "In any future war, the army would have to look in every groundhog hole in the state to find me."

Charles' death was a crisis for me. I wrote to the draft board and asked to be reclassified so I could serve in the Navy, but they would not change it. Meanwhile, I was losing some of my idealism and beginning to develop a social conscience. I had heard we were developing super bombs and I had powerful, mixed feelings about this. My commitment to the ministry was weakening. I had to sort things out.

We were all devastated by my brother's loss but my mother most of all. She went into a deep depression that went on for two years. She had a best friend in Moorefield, Mrs. Friddle. When Mrs. Friddle lost her son from a rare disease, Mother came out of her depression—her friend needed her.

My younger brother, Rodney, was another story. He grew to be six feet one and was drafted his senior year of high school. He spent four years at the Great Lakes training center as a male nurse. When he was discharged, he entered a wild period. He and Dad were always in conflict and now things became worse. His savings from his days in the service soon disappeared in drink at the local American Legion club and his bills went unpaid. He would have allowed his G.I. insurance to lapse when the $10,000 policy was almost paid up, but Dad could not allow it and picked up the remaining payments. He expected Rodney would inform him when he cashed in his policy so he could pay his debt. It never happened.

Dad began to lose complete trust in his son. Rodney worked in Father's insurance agency for a time, but he was not responsible. He had enrolled in several colleges and failed. Then he met Marilyn, a beautiful, sexy woman who was flirtatious and had a violent temper. She was attracted to Rodney, a handsome guy, and set out to marry him. She succeeded, they married and had two sons; two others were stillborn. Then Marilyn fell in love with a member of the Marine Band and took off with him and the two boys to Rochester, New York. She prevented Rodney from seeing his sons until they were in their teens. She told the older boy that if he tried to look up his grandmother, she would disown him. This grandchild later became the reconciler in family rifts.

During the Korean War, Rodney was recalled for a second four-year tour at Great Lakes.

Chapter 8

Boston

Graduate school in Boston was an exciting place to be. The university had twenty-five schools spread about the city and was now developing a new campus on Commonwealth Avenue. Everyone had a story about the president, Danny Marsh, and his ability to raise money. In one such tale, the Stone brothers offered to give a half million dollars to build a science building if it was named for them. The board was elated at the news until Danny informed them the building would cost a million and a half. When he told one of the brothers he couldn't do it for less than the full amount, the man called his brother and they decided yes. And so today the science building is named for the Stone brothers.

My professor of religion was Dr. Edgar Brightman. I had many conferences with him, never sitting but walking at a brisk pace, accompanying him from the old school of theology on Mt. Vernon Street to the new campus on Commonwealth Avenue. One of the most popular teachers in the theological school was Edward Prince Booth, a spellbinder, who taught through the use of biographies. On occasion, he was known to serve wine to his students in class. He's the one who said, "If you think that Jesus and his followers did not drink wine, try taking a drink of water out of a goatskin that has traveled two weeks in the scorching desert sun. The limited amount of alcohol preserved the water."

I was always scrambling from school to job to another job, then back to school. I was first employed at the Wilbur restaurant at the bottom of the hill. Fay Gemmell worked at Wilbur's and asked about a job for me. So I worked the noon meal until Chris and I were married. It was not my favorite restaurant. We sometimes had to fight to get what a customer had ordered and, worse, we'd watch the chef throw whole chickens, pin feathers and all, into a pot in preparing southern fried chicken, the restaurant specialty. I suddenly did not have much appetite for fried chicken.

I was also a waiter in the Patten restaurant in Scollay Square and the Ambassador on Winter Street. The Ambassador was across the street from the jewelry store where I bought a diamond for Chris. Mr. Long, the owner, was known to loan money to theological students for their purchases. I went to see him and ended up borrowing $75 to buy the ring, and agreed to pay it off in a year. The next year when I went to pay him back, he said, "I don't need the $75. It's a gift with the condition that when you have more money in the future, you will assist another student." Amazing.

The manager of the Ambassador was another gem, the opposite of his name, Mr. Savage. He would do anything for his employees, including allow us to order steak when it was at a premium. The war was over and shortages were everywhere. The irony of the three restaurants is that the Wilbur was the only one that survived and it eventually signed the food contract at the new campus of BU.

I continued to do different jobs in the summer but began focusing on young people to develop skills that would help me in my ministry. One summer I worked as a camp counselor to two very different groups of boys, black boys from Roxbury and white boys from Lexington. They were "lockouts," meaning both parents worked and the kids were locked out of their homes until their parents returned. The two groups were competitors in basketball and I coached both teams.

After practice one afternoon, the black team broke into the candy machines in the lobby and took both the money and the candy. We caught them red-handed. The director asked for a meeting with the boys after they had made restitution. He asked the team leader to stand before the team while the director took some string from his pocket. He asked the boy to hold his hands together. The director then tied the boy's hands and asked him if he could break the string. He did, easily. Then the director tied his hands twice. It was still easy to break the string. By the fifth round of string, he could not break it.

The director explained to them a bad habit was like the string. Each repeat would bind them in bad behavior. Well, it must have worked for some. I never had another negative incident with the boys from Roxbury. They went on to win the basketball championship. But it didn't work for everybody. Several years later, I had occasion to meet one of the boys from the Lexington group. He had become a lawyer and was being disbarred for stealing money from his clients' accounts.

One never knows what effect such lessons will have on kids. I think a few learned something that day. Whatever path they took, I believe they all remember that piece of string.

The next summer, I was hired by the Huntington Avenue YMCA to be a counselor at Camp Beckett on Lake Rudd in Lee, Massachusetts, in the heart of the Berkshires. Camp Beckett owned 350 wonderful acres of land and I was elated to discover there was no poison ivy and no poison snakes. The boys could explore the woods freely in their assigned areas. The camp was organized around age groups and my group, the eight to ten-year-olds, lived in Abernicki Village with its own territory and swimming area.

Lake Rudd stood at the highest elevation in the state and the water was briskly cold. My job was to teach swimming to my group of kids. The director knew I was a good swimmer but lacked experience in teaching swimming skills so I learned as I went along. I soon realized that five boys had deep aversions to water, and this was a real problem because, of course, they had to put their faces underwater to do the crawl. It was a challenge, but I had a teaching prop, a heavy stone the boys could not pick up. It was placed in the water and they had to bring it up. They were all Supermen, wanting to be first, and they forgot their fears and went under.

It worked for everyone except one lad who, when he heard the bugle call for swimming would disappear into that 350 acres of land. He reappeared when swimming was over. He was a great challenge to the swimming staff, and eventually we learned the source of his problem. He had an older sister, also at the camp, whose message to the world was—*take him back, sell him, kill him. I do not want a baby brother.* On several occasions she had pushed him under the water and held him down. It was one of the most intense cases of sibling rivalry one could imagine. We did not succeed in getting him to enter the swimming area the entire month he was at camp, but we made an effort to counsel his sister.

I did get to know a father of one of the boys, briefly. His son was a clinger, always hanging around me, and one of the five that required special attention. When his father came for parents' weekend, he gave his son a box of Milky Ways, two dozen bars, then wandered off to show the boy's friends the chocolate treats. The son's face immediately dropped and his father could not see his look of disappointment. The boy had waited all week to show his father his creations from arts and crafts class. The father finally got it when I told him that a visit to the craft area was worth more than 24 candy bars.

One of the most popular events was the fish fry. As a fisherman, I was well aware the lake was loaded with small bass, pickerel and pike, and I helped the campers learn how to fish. Mostly the catch was small and the fish were thrown back. But preparing for the fish fry was different. Instead of returning the catch to the lake, they were cleaned and frozen until there were enough to feed the whole camp. One of the campers actually landed a six-pound pike.

The previous summer the camp had been hard hit by an epidemic of polio. Some 24 campers and four staff had come down with it, including the camp director's son. Four had died. It was thought that fatigue had something to do with developing the disease so all the campers this year had to lie down on their backs for an hour after lunch. During that summer, the camp had only four cases of polio.

All of these summer jobs helped me later in working with youth in my ministry.

Chapter 9

Marriage

While on vacation back in Moorefield, I needed to return some items to Christine so I called her and she agreed to see me in Morgantown. She knew I had lost my brother and I believed she was being kind and wanted to offer her sympathy. But it was more than that. We went out to "Sam's Place" and in the course of our conversation, we reconciled. I knew it was Chris I really wanted all along. We wrote furiously to each other after this and her letters were really poetic. We became more and more in love.

Two special moments made me realize Chris and I would marry. One was back in West Virginia the day I carried her across the Potomac River—she weighed only 89 pounds at the time. We climbed a hill on the other side and had a picnic on the bluff. We were full of each other and everything was right—the weather, the food, the usual worries about goals and careers put on hold. The moment was so perfect I can almost reach out and touch it, over a half-century later.

The second moment was when Chris spent Thanksgiving weekend in Boston and everything was perfect again. She stayed with my best friends, the Gemmell's, and they showed us how a beautiful marriage worked. They were wonderful role models and their example enabled us to see that we could do it too. We really could get married while I was in school just as they had. Now we had one question left: How would Chris handle being a minister's wife? Her heart was with art and she feared this great passion of hers would be sucked up by her wifely duties. She was determined not to let this happen.

She also wanted to marry me. When? As soon as possible.

I called her family on Thanksgiving Day and said with great excitement, "Get ready, we're getting married the day after Christmas." And so we were married on December 26, 1945. The timing was strange but true. I now had two years of theological school under my belt and Chris was still teaching in Cincinnati. She had signed a teaching contract she had to fulfill through the winter term and I would continue as a student. We would marry, go our separate ways for a few months, be together in Boston, then together always.

The wedding was in Morgantown on the day of a huge snowstorm. Between Moorefield and Morgantown are three brutal mountain ranges. I was in Moorefield for Christmas and the next day we took off for my wedding in Morgantown. We drove in one car—my parents, my brother Rodney, and I. We had to drive over the mountains and through this blinding snowstorm—we were four hours late getting there and lucky to get there at all. But they couldn't have the wedding without the groom.

We limped into town on a snowdrift and Christine and I were married at the Morgantown Methodist Church. Bill Keefe, my roommate who was also from West Virginia, was the only friend who made it across the icy mountain ranges. He had offered to take pictures of the wedding and discovered later that his camera was not working and so—no pictures.

After the wedding, we waited for four hours in Grafton for a train to take us to Clarksburg. Grafton was a dirty town because it was the center for coke production used in the making of steel. Large amounts of soft coal were used to fuel the double engines that pulled the loaded train cars up and down the Allegheny Front. The area towns were surrounded by coke ovens that gave off a thick black smoke that kept the sun in a haze. It was still snowing when we boarded the train to Clarksburg and we went right to our hotel.

We had a hilarious moment when I opened my suitcase and, behold, it was filled with my grandmother's clothes (and her bottle of whiskey.) Our suitcases had been switched so I had a honeymoon with no underwear. It was as good a time as ever to make that mistake! Christine returned to Cincinnati to finish her term and I went back to Boston to my classes.

And, oh, Chris's mother eventually made out a schedule for me to meet the relatives. I looked at it and quietly groaned. It would take forever and I balked at the thought of meeting relatives in such a formal way. I suggested a big open house to see them all in one shot, and then we could all play bridge. So that's what we did. We talked and ate and played bridge—everybody played, and we were all happy with this resolution.

Married Life in Boston

I often felt I had gone from the beauty of West Virginia to the worst of Boston. Oh, I know Boston is beautiful, but sometimes that depends on your living conditions and the state of your wallet. I had moved to a second floor, three-room apartment that would accommodate Chris, on the Scollay Square side of Beacon Hill, the seedy heart of Boston. I quickly discovered it was noisy, dirty, crowded and smelly. Seven different languages were spoken in the apartments on Garden Street.

That spring Christine joined me in Boston and she tried to be a good sport about our living conditions. Let me put it this way: The living was awful but our cultural life was magnificent. Our building was old and infested with every kind of vermin—mice, rats, cockroaches and bed bugs. DDT became our best friend and we used it heavily for two years. (I now think it was responsible for my Parkinson's.) We were constantly spraying the mattress.

But pesticides couldn't do everything. We both screamed when a half-grown mouse jumped from under my pillow one night. I thought I had plugged up every possible entrance but he found a way. We chased it through the apartment before Chris picked up a "Life Magazine" and whopped it with a fierce blow. Then she cried for two hours for having killed the little creature. I also suspect she was crying over the situation she was in. Cleanliness was next to godliness for her.

The contrast of the bustle and mad haste of the city with our rural background in West Virginia was striking. We had truly left the country behind and entered a new land, but the city had its quirks and beauties too. Christine soon got a job as an artist with Taylor Company, a shop that made window displays out of paper mache for Jordan Marsh and Filenes. This was the time when "Make Way for Ducklings" became a popular children's book and we felt like the book was all about us that summer as we walked arm in arm through the Boston Common and Gardens.

One of the story's most memorable characters is the policeman who directs traffic at the corner of Beacon and Boylston Street, halting it until Mother Mallard and her ducklings make their way to and from Boston Common. He directs the traffic with the flourish of an orchestra conductor and Boston used it to advantage, featuring him in the ads to lure tourists here. There were such characters aplenty in Boston, and we loved the charm and diversity and liveliness of the street life. Life indoors was another matter. The noise from the first and third floors told us that serious alcoholics lived there. And one day we met a rat coming up the stairs as we were going down. But in that other world, we heard great symphonies, operas, lectures.

Our very best friends were the Gemmells, from Nebraska, the couple Chris had stayed with on that special Thanksgiving weekend. We would be friends with the Gemmells for life. Fay decided to major in psychology under Dr. Paul Johnson. I was more interested in sociology and majored under Dr. Walter Mulder in social ethics. Eventually Fay was awarded his doctorate. I never finished because I could not prove my thesis. But that's a story for later. Both Fay and I served five small Methodist churches over a period of twenty years. Then our lives took a different, but similar, direction.

Fay was a member of the Seminary Singers, which included 36 men, a soprano and an organist. Fay talked me into trying out and I was accepted partly because I could sing bass. A spring tour was planned and we would sing 37 concerts in six weeks. Christine would be left alone in Boston.

The organist for the Seminary Singers was Richard Elsasers, a student at BU Theological. He was widely known for his glorious playing; he played with every major orchestra in the country and on every major organ, even the great organ in the Mormon temple in Salt Lake City. He knew all of Bach's organ works by memory (which would take him two weeks to play). Richard loved being on the road.

Enrolling as a student had been his way of escaping the draft, he said, and we never knew whether to believe him. He definitely did not fit the mold; he was gay and sometimes took speed to keep going. But then, lots of students took speed, even in those innocent days.

The tour was great fun and a great education, but it had its moments. Richard was unpredictable whenever he became upset with the director, Dr. James Houghton. One concert was held in a Chicago theatre at the last minute because of an overflow audience. Richard was supposed to sound the high C for the beginning of Palestrina's "Tenebrae." He hit a cowbell instead.

One day our bus broke down in the Arizona desert and Richard decided to take a hike. He walked so far, pushed along by the thin dry air, he could not get back in time and when he finally did he was badly sunburned. While we had been waiting and goofing around, we discovered several red-ant hills and kicked the sides in before we got back on the bus. Our soprano was critical of our behavior. As the bus started up, she screamed and ran up to the driver. He said, "Eyes front, gentlemen." She went to the back of the bus to remove the ants (I dared not ask where they were.) Altogether, we lost two days and had to drive a thousand miles without stopping to make Los Angeles on time to give four concerts (and stay within our budget.)

The tour was an eye-opener in other ways. In Kansas City, Missouri, in 90-degree heat, I was shocked to see Mexican children standing on the fence of the town swimming pool watching, as they were barred from swimming. In Flagstaff, Arizona, we stopped to have a major meal. Most of us had ordered soup as a first course when the owners noticed our two black members and said they were not welcome. We stated quite clearly they were members of our party. But, no. They could not be served. We left on that long trek to LA without food. We felt terrible for the men, and I was having a growing feeling that breaking up the caste system had to be part of my life's work.

I have in my possession a letter I wrote to Chris at the beginning of our tour. It was written in Syracuse, New York.

My Darling Wife,

This is not a diary, honey, but a love letter because I sure am going to miss you. I love you so much that leaving you is a job I hope will never be necessary again. I'm sure I am not all there without you. My better self is gone.

The concert tonight was wonderful! Going on tour does something (to the music). I walked the mountaintop during the whole concert, tired though I was.

Tomorrow we see Niagara Falls and I'll be thinking of you. Just now it is 11 p.m. and I am saying a little prayer—Father in heaven who has given us our love, keep it beautiful and strong that we may grow into two more noble people because of it. Protect my beloved and guard her as I would. Grant her peace of mind and joy in all she does. Tell her I love her more each day and even now look to the day when she will be once more in my arms.

Write me, won't you darling. I will need your letters to give me extra stamina for this trip.

I love you, darling. I adore you.

All my love,

Beanie

The summer of 1948 Chris and I embarked on a crazy trip, a trip that was supposed to be six weeks but was cut short. Chris has two sisters. Her younger sister Edie married a nice guy, Bill Wilson, the wealthy owner of a Ford franchise. In fact, I married them. Their marriage was one of the social events of the year with seven bridesmaids and a reception at the Fairmont Country Club. For a wedding gift, the family financed a trip for the couple to the West Coast to tour the national parks. All of them. Edie and Bill invited us to come along.

As it happened, there was a catch to the road trip. Bill's younger sister Joyce was involved in a bad romance, and her parents wanted to put an end to it so they arranged for her to go on the trip too. Distance and time was sure to end the relationship, they thought. Wilson-Ford of the Ford franchise would provide the car and we would pay some of the expenses, an important matter to us in those days.

Visiting all the national parks was an ambitious undertaking. The first day we drove from Fairmont, West Virginia to the Grand Teton National Park in Wyoming. Bill drove all the way and did not stop even once, regardless of the discomfort of his passengers. Finally we pulled into the Grand Teton campground and, lo and behold, the place was in an uproar. Two young climbers had fallen on an ice field and one had suffered a broken leg. A rescue party was being organized and we felt this awful sense of emergency. Watching this near-tragedy unfold, Bill calmed down, directed the setting up of our tents, and we put together a meal. Joyce was somewhat indifferent to all this. She had no interest in going on this trip with us. She felt she was a hostage.

We crawled into our tents looking for some much-needed sleep. But that evening a bear cub got lost, climbed a pine tree and cried its heart out for its mother. It was an eerie, heartbreaking sound, almost like a human voice and our nerves were shattered. Before daylight it started to rain. When Bill zipped open his tent to check the weather, the noise awakened the girls. They screamed, "Help! There's a bear trying to get in our tent." And they really thought so too.

Then Edie threw up. We soon discovered that Edie was pregnant and she began throwing up every morning and noon. Apparently her family had known she was pregnant before we left but they felt she should go anyway. No one on the trip, including her husband Bill, knew of her condition. So now we were in a situation. We traveled on, heading for the Los Angeles suburb where the third McMillen sister, Jean, lived with her husband, Ed. He was an engineer for Lockheed and a member of the "Skunk Works," the five men team that designed warplanes. We stayed several days to give Edie time to recover. By this time she was not only miserable but had lost considerable weight.

We did have some memorable moments though. Ed and Jean's five-year-old son was a delight and I spent time listening to him describe the latest plane his father had designed. But Edie was not improving and we had concern now for the safety of both mother and child. We made a decision to go home and miss the second half of our trip. When we arrived in Fairmont, Edie was hospitalized with dehydration. She had lost a lot of weight.

As for Joyce's romance, it ended—she married someone else her parents didn't approve of. As a result, she was disinherited from the family, which was probably a good thing—they were far too controlling.

Meanwhile, back in Moorefield, my father had a new job. The richest man in Moorefield was M. A. Bean, who owned the first Ford dealership, the first gas distribution business, the filling stations and half the town. We Beans were not related to him, but when his accountant died, Dad was hired as business manager to take his place. The hapless accountant never asked for a raise in 30 years and got none. M. A. Bean was a pillar in the Methodist Church and particularly active in the men's Bible class. He always said, "Business is business and religion is religion. The two cannot mix." I went fishing with him because he needed someone to row the boat while he cast for bass. We often discussed religion.

When his repair shop foreman of 25 years had a kidney stone removed and could not physically return to work, M.A. fired him. The man died, but to his credit M.A. paid his daughter's college expenses. So you might say he did mix business and religion, at least this time. The new job was a big responsibility for Dad.

My studies at BU that eventually earned me the STB degree (Bachelor of Sacred Theology) were based on the work of Swedish sociologist Gunnar Myrdal. His 1500-page book, "The American Dilemma," was our bible, and many of those pages analyzed the social dynamics that were at work destroying the American caste system. The most compelling social pressures on black/white communities to change were in fact very similar, but the importance of each facet was in reverse order. Myrdal calls this the Rank Order of Discrimination and it is the heart of the study.

Social issues were of most importance to whites, objecting as they did to intermarriage between the races and adhering to stringent unwritten rules in social intercourse—rules revolving around everyday conversation and interaction between blacks and whites. Jobs and education for blacks were of less importance. Conversely, for the black community, the most important force for improvement was employment and the second was education. The list continued in reverse order ending with intermarrying between the races.

After two years, I still had to complete some course work and begin my journey toward a Ph.D., but that summer I got my feet wet by becoming the youth director at the Methodist Church in Lynn, Massachusetts working under the church's minister, Rev. Boutwell. Actually Christine and I shared the position, which included planning youth activities, worship services and teaching a Sunday school class. For this we were paid $25 a week.

Methodist churches in New England are small and, in most cases, too small to support a fulltime pastor. On top of this, Protestant churches in general were losing members to the suburbs. In the fall of 1948, I began the grueling job of serving a parish full-time on a part-time salary and continuing my long journey toward a Ph.D.

Chapter 10

The Peabody Methodist Church (1947-1950)

I have always considered the people who belonged to the Peabody Church the best thing that could have happened to us. They welcomed this green and untried pastor as their own and trained us (yes, Chris, too) during the three years we were there. The church, located on Boston's North Shore, had about 200 members and I had a hard act to follow. My predecessor was Jim Laird, a brilliant speaker and preacher but fortunately, I was accepted for who I was. The truth was it would be a while before I knew who I was myself.

In those days, and probably in many churches today, when you hire a pastor you also get the pastor's wife. It was simply expected. I explained to the interviewing committee that Chris would not be the traditional pastor's wife. Her goal was to be an artist, and her well being depended on it. They accepted this, but life intervened in our plans. Chris became a mother first.

Events that were to shape my life occurred during our Peabody years. Our first son Charles was born in Salem Hospital. I became adept at performing weddings and funerals. I learned how to work with individuals and groups. In short, this church offered me the ideal student ministry.

The church building fronted on Main Street, a plain structure that needed a good coat of paint and the parsonage was nearby on Sewell. It had ten rooms, quite a contrast to our little Boston apartment. The parsonage came with the job; we did not have to pay rent.

One of the features of the church was a large chandelier with twenty light bulbs, every one of them brown with age. I wanted to change them, but the janitor objected, saying it was almost impossible to reach them even with the long ladder stored in the church. It would require two strong men to hold the ladder, he said, and it would be dangerous. The bulbs had been there over two decades and he had never replaced one. New ones would need to be constantly replaced. I have the feeling the old brown bulbs still serve.

As a pastor, I was on the liberal side though Methodism has strong roots in social action and I fit well into this picture. Racial justice, labor rights, equality of women, civil rights—all were very Methodist. Our hymns celebrate social welfare. Personally, I wanted to see the end of the black/white caste system more than most, perhaps because I was still haunted by those black figures of my youth—Fanny and Louis. I was not a ranting, raving minister; rather I spoke softly and carried no stick. Even then, some people would walk out of the church rather than hear what I had to say. But then, people don't have to agree with their pastors. I ask only that their minds be open. Fortunately, enough people sat with minds open and stayed put.

The Methodist parsonage was next door to the Episcopal parsonage and I quickly became friends with the pastor, a former Methodist, who had attended Boston University before becoming an Episcopalian. He enlightened me about the theological split in the Episcopal church, somewhere between high church and liberal reform.

Every Sunday he sent flowers from his 8 a.m. service to my 11 a.m. service, provided I would announce they were in memory of John Wesley, a man who had always remained a good Anglican. My new friend was a liberal, in stark contrast to his predecessor, an Anglo-Catholic priest whose service was a Mass—very Catholic really. The only thing missing was loyalty to the pope.

The new rector set out to change the image of his church in the community and he invited me to exchange pulpits. We participated in union services and I was invited to speak briefly at the 75th anniversary of his church. The bishop was there along with the former priest. I have the feeling they were shocked.

We had a harsh winter that first year. I remember complaining to Christine about the lack of snow as we started for West Virginia for Christmas. We went back home about twice a year, at Christmas and in the summer. In New England we learned that things change quickly. While we were gone, a foot of slush fell and froze. It snowed the rest of the winter and I watched the fence posts in front of the house disappear.

We had over six feet of snow on the ground before spring arrived to melt it. We never got the car in the shed.

It was here in Peabody that I experienced the most pressure I'd ever felt in my life, culminating with a week from hell. I was still a student at BU finishing my residence courses and exams were upon me. Chris was expecting a baby, which was wonderful but for the timing, in May. Meanwhile, the Annual New England Methodist Conference was being held in Worcester and pastors and church officials were required to be there every day. I was being ordained at the Sunday service and had to prepare; the ordination would make me an official pastor. So I had a baby, final exams and my ordination in a single week.

A terrible time for my car to break down but there it was. I was driving to Worcester and back everyday in my old car and I heard a groaning, then bump-bump-bump... I pulled over and saw that one of the old worn-out tires had a balloon sticking out the side of it. I had to replace the tire at the worst possible moment, when time and money were short.

Baby Charles arrived on May 20, 1949, when I was taking my final exams at BU. Christine's friend had talked her into going to the hospital at the first sign of a labor pain. And so she did, but it was a full 24 hours before real labor took place. As it turned out, I was in the middle of a final during the blessed event. In those days, fathers were not welcome in the labor room or at the birth. I was told that I should watch my wife for depression on the third day after birth, and I resolved to remember this. The hospital limited the number and time that friends and family could visit patients. What a peculiar position I was in—I could visit anybody as a pastor but could not visit my own wife until that evening.

At this point, I made a terrible mistake. A parishioner invited me to go trout fishing and though I felt a little guilty I was desperate for a break. Where else, but the Merrimack River? I caught a nice rainbow trout and stayed too long trying to catch another, then realized it was too late to visit Christine. To make things worse, the nurse who told Chris that I had gone fishing was one of the hospital's most beautiful volunteers. Imagine how Chris felt! She was exhausted and rumpled and desperate for my support and this movie star tells her that her husband is off fishing. Christine's anger and disappointment persisted and, honestly, I don't think she's over that one yet. It was inexcusable of me.

It was a bad time for a major gaffe in other ways too. Christine and I were making a success of our marriage in spite of our different life goals. We had shared a lot of pain over the Episcopal rector's plight; the poor guy was engaged and just days before the wedding, his fiancé called it off and left town. All the plans had been made, the invitations sent out. Now the rector felt not only loss but embarrassment too as the whole town chattered. Our neighbor's grief drew Christine and I closer. Now I had made a mess of things—over a trout that got away.

Baby Charles was a blessing. A beautiful baby, of course, and good-natured. Everyone spoiled him. Fortunately, my mother had come from West Virginia to care for Chris and the baby. I tried to be helpful but, in fact, I was not at home enough. The demands of a church of 200 were overwhelming for this neophyte and I took on other people's problems because I didn't know how not to. I was counseling church members at this point, and it was my good fortune to be under the supervision of Dr. John Green at BU. Dr. Green was a pioneer in counseling and marital education. Eventually I too would teach Marriage and the Family; I was lucky to have such a fine mentor and supervisor.

Parish life was lively and a good deal was going on in town. The Mothers Club in Peabody asked me to install their newly elected officers. A very pregnant Mrs. Bruce was present and she left early because she was having labor pains. She gave birth that night. Two days later I went to the hospital to see her and when I entered her room it was not the Mrs. Bruce I was looking for. I found the correct Mrs. Bruce in the Salem Hospital. Two Mrs. Bruce's giving birth the same night!

A group of parishioners put on a play called "Aaron Slick from Pumpkin Crick." Chris was invited to play the role of the country bumpkin who taught the city slicker a thing or two, and she was game. She had always been somewhat shy and people were surprised to see her dramatic performance. The play was so successful we later performed a comedy in which an actor handed a twenty-five pound chunk of ice to the person sitting on an aisle seat. The actor said, "Pass it on." At that moment, a lady jumped up from her seat, shouting as she rushed out, "Oh, my God, I left my baby in Filene's Basement!"

The Protestant churches in Peabody participated in a campaign called The Every Member Canvass, and a good thing it turned out to be. The churches recruited a number of parishioners, trained them, supplied materials, developed publicity and hired an inspirational speaker to get them committed and excited. On a designated Sunday evening, they visited the homes of members to get them to pledge to the church. It proved to be a successful way to raise money.

Life on the home front was full of small dramas. Christine was allergic to ragweed, cats and a litany of things. August and September were the worst for her and the first frost usually brought an end to her suffering. Not this year—as we managed to acquire two parsonage cats. On a cold day in February as I walked past the home of the Episcopal rector I heard the faint mewing of kittens coming from the far corner of the house under the porch. They were suddenly silent when I tried to coax them out. I crawled under the porch and caught them, half-frozen, dirty and unfriendly, hissing and mewing their distrust.

Christine was not exactly happy about adopting two alley cats but knew they would die if put out in the cold. So we kept them in. They went out in the spring and, as adults, they owned the world. They did not allow any wandering dog or cat to come into our yard. A boy who lived up the street said his dog would teach those cats a lesson and he brought his dog over. One cat was sitting on the front step and the other was on the fence. When the dog saw two cats, he slowed up a little, then headed straight for the cat on the step, leaving his backside exposed. The cat on the fence jumped on his back and rode the dog out of the yard, howling and scratching. The cat on the step sat there watching, ready to take action if necessary. Soon after, one cat was hit by a car and the other simply left.

In so many ways, Peabody is still with us. Soon after we arrived, I performed my very first marriage and we are still in touch with the bride and groom. Robert and Phyllis Manoogian recently called to say they were making the trip from Peabody to Dartmouth to celebrate their 50th wedding anniversary. Robert and I reminisced about our first camping trip together with Chris and Phyl on Mt. Washington when we set up our pup tent and forgot to dig a trench around it. The rain came down in torrents and we were sodden. Robert was the son of a doctor and his mother was famous in the Armenian community for her cooking. No way could Phyllis compete with her mother-in-law in the kitchen, and we still laughed about that.

I have nothing but good memories of Peabody, but after three years serving the church, from 1947 to 1950, it was time to move on. The Methodist Church moved its pastors along every two or three years.

The annual New England Methodist Conference was coming up. At this time, the church leadership was powerful. A bishop presided over each Conference, and each district within the Conference was ruled by a superintendent. The weeklong Conference of hundreds was devoted to reporting from the different churches, discussing political and social issues, and it was also a kind of job fare. A pastor would be assigned to his next church right here, following a meeting between the bishop, the superintendent, a layperson from the prospective church, and the pastor. Obviously a lot of preliminary work took place before the Conference.

I had been ordained a deacon, which made me an elder and earned me membership in the Conference. The structure is similar to the Church of England under John Wesley. The Methodists formed a Federation for Social Action, which serves as an actual seminary. Methodists believe that what you do is more important than what you think and they put their money and their voices in support of social action and education.

Chapter 11

Bradford

From Peabody, I was assigned to the Methodist church in Bradford, a suburb of Haverhill, north of Boston. It sat on the banks of the Merrimack River, which travels about twelve miles through the city. Bradford itself refers to the area of Haverhill on the south side of the river and the proximity of the river was not lost on this fisherman. It was as if I'd said, "Please, just a nice little church on a fish-filled river." And there it was.

The parsonage at Bradford was a mini-mansion with twelve rooms and an entrance with a beautiful stairway. The house required 30 tons of coal a year to heat. We blocked off most of the rooms and turned the dining room into the living room. My office was on the second floor. The church was a wooden structure that needed painting. One Saturday shortly after I arrived, twenty men showed up with paintbrushes. I was assigned to paint the gable.

The parishioners were almost all working class, cobbling together shoes in the local factory. Bradford began as a town of sawmills and gristmills, powered by the river and was now known for its shoes. In the small congregation of 150, there was one professional, a CEO from the local gas company and the treasurer of the church. It was a church of young couples and, lucky for me, the people were eager to serve.

Leaders stepped forward to form a Mothers Club; they taught Sunday school and led a Sunday evening youth group. The first conflict arose when the youth advisers wanted to sponsor a square dance as part of a total youth program. I worked with a devoted but fundamentalist superintendent who agreed with the Methodist church's negative stance on dancing, going back to the days when we were all farmers.

Dancing was a source of sin and a waste of energy. Why waste your energy dancing when you have to wake up and do hard physical labor? But times were changing. Industry had replaced the plow long ago and now labor saving devices were invading American life. The young were not getting enough physical exercise, and a new day required a new response. I thought the time had come for dancing and, to my surprise, the superintendent agreed. It was a big day when dancing became part of the youth program.

"Just don't ask *me* to dance," I warned them.

The support group for young parents was one of the most popular, and both Chris and I were part of it. On one occasion, the wives were assigned to come to the meeting armed with a story about their husbands. Each couple had to give "good reasons" why they had married each other. As the pastor, I went first and made my case.

"When I first met Chris, she had money in the bank, designed and made her own clothes, she had her silver, and her mother made the best pecan rolls I had ever eaten."

Chris castigated me for being so preoccupied with things and was quiet. Then when her turn came to say why she married me, she made her case, briefly.

"Well, I was desperate," she said. Though she was shy and lacked self-confidence, she was full of surprises and the group loved it. She got a standing ovation.

The parsonage was on a busy street and that became a problem. Charles was old enough to play outdoors and there was no fence to keep him from going in the street. The Gemmells, now serving a church in Lawrence, had a fence, which relieved Fay and Charlotte from non-stop child watching. We, too, wanted a fence but had no money and the play space was ridiculously small anyway. Since we could not put our son behind a fence, we decided to put the fence in the child. We set limits on how far up and down the street Charles could go. If he went in the street, he was instantly banished to the house.

"This is as far as I can go," he told the elderly gentleman who often passed by and spoiled him rotten.

We knew we were making progress. The crack in the sidewalk marked the limit. Meanwhile, the Gemmells were having a different sort of problem. Little John had climbed over their fence and the police found him ten blocks from home. Their German Shepherd dog that had been trained to grab John and pull him back on the sidewalk had accompanied him on his little journey.

I'd only been in Bradford two weeks when a man named Francois Bouquet knocked on the door. He said he had a job picking apples waiting for him in New Hampshire and he needed money for a bus ticket. I believed him and gave him $10. The next morning he called and said the apples were further north and he needed more money to make the trip.

"No more," I told him.

In the meantime I called Fay Gemmell and asked his advice. Ministers do a lot of kibitzing and he already knew about Francois. He seemed surprised no one had told me—the man was a pro at getting money from new clergy. That day, he rang the doorbell again and Christine answered. He flew by her up the stairs to my office. I looked him in the eye and asked him if he knew Reverend Gemmell in Lawrence. Without a word, he ran out as fast as he had run in.

Two weeks before Christmas, a man came into the church and said,

"You probably will not believe me but I need 50 cents to buy a bottle of wine to get drunk. A judge in Marblehead will sentence me for six months and I need to get home for Christmas. I have been in and out of the Middleton Prison farm for 28 years—it is my home."

I was able to confirm his story and so, for better or worse, I gave him the 50 cents.

We had a family in the church whose 12-year-old daughter was into random sex with multiple partners anywhere and everywhere. Her mother had many children and did not pay any attention to who was coming and going from her house at night. The girl's reputation was spreading and she was heading for worse trouble. I was asked to counsel the family and put it back together, but my previous experience already told me the truth. If a family falls apart, there is almost no way to put it back together. This family was broken. The girl went to a foster home and that is how we solved the matter.

The Kinsey Report had come out with its report investigating the sexual habits of Americans and the country was shocked. Homosexuality was hinted at in the ranks of ministers, teachers and other professionals. Sex had been a taboo subject for so long, no one knew what to think. Many wanted to put it right back in the box. Being a counselor, I heard a lot about taboo subjects. In the counseling office you find out what is really going on.

One of our babysitters was Mrs. Cram who delighted to get her hands on Charles and loved babysitting for us. No one in the neighborhood knew how old she was and she told no one. Then one day she had a heart attack and was near death. I was sitting with her when the neighbors came in to see how she was doing. She had been unconscious for hours. We were discussing her age when she opened her eyes and said, "I'm 88!" And then she closed her eyes. She recovered and smiled about having revealed her secret.

I joined the Kiwanis Club in Haverhill; it was a new experience for me, associating with business people. I did not have good feelings about business mostly due to my father's experiences. As a businessman himself, he was constantly bilked by prominent people in town, even his own partner. People didn't keep their word. I picked up his attitudes and had a built-in distrust of the business world. But as a pastor, I felt it was important for me to reach out—it was good for me to know different kinds of people and get a larger view.

The Kiwanis was the most active, hardest-working, hardest-drinking and best-liked group in town. The club paid for my membership when I agreed to publish a weekly newsletter that was mailed to members. The president was a professional entertainer and I became good friends with him and his wife. When Tim developed a cancer of the stomach and was given only a few months to live, he asked me to talk to his wife and give her the bad news. I said this was a task for his priest but he said, no, he had no personal relationship with his priest.

Most of our neighbors were Catholics and interesting people. Our neighbor up the street was a chemist working on new ways to control flies at racetracks. He discovered that flies had developed new strains resistant to DDT so he had to be creative. Our back doors opened to each other and we had many conversations about this and other things. He had two daughters and the older was retarded, the sweetest child you could ever meet. The younger was three and her dad spent a lot of time teaching her to memorize Hiawatha.

Across the street lived a young lady who had married a Catholic and signed a pledge that she would raise their children as Catholics. She gave birth to a son and two years later, two priests came to her house asking if she was using birth control, which would be a no, no. They assumed she must be because she was not pregnant again. One of the Catholic churches in town was liberal and the other very conservative. I assume she and her husband were attending the conservative one. The whole neighborhood heard about it.

Though I don't drink alcohol, I break my self-imposed rule when I am the guest for a Seder meal in a Jewish family, but that's about it. I don't believe in advertising alcohol either and have campaigned against it. Also, the church took a strong stand. In those days, you were not allowed to join the Methodist church if you drank alcohol. So imagine my consternation when I caught the largest striper in a fishing contest and won a case of beer. I did not know what to do with it.

I went to the package store to see if I could return it, but they wouldn't take it. So I put it in the trunk of my car and carried it around with me for several weeks trying to figure out what to do. Sometimes I forgot it was there. Other times I feared I would open my trunk and some of my parishioners would see it and I'd be in trouble with the bishop. I wondered if I could give it to the Kiwanis Club, but I had counseled a number of people there to help them stop drinking so, no. One night I went casting at the Plum Island spot where the Merrimack enters the ocean. I stopped on the bridge and threw the case of beer in the river.

Our second son James was born at the Haverhill Hospital, just 22 months younger than Charles. I'd like to say this part is about James but it is not. Our firstborn Charles was a happy baby until James came along. He became very unhappy any time we attended to James' needs and, in general, his behavior deteriorated. The reason why struck me like a bolt of lightning. Charles did not want a baby brother and, though just a toddler himself, he could verbalize his feelings of rage at having to share his world.

Where once he was king, now he had been dethroned, and we all felt the stress of his behavior. He would punch, bite and hit James until he cried. Naturally we intervened, but the behavior continued. Charles asked us to give him away, sell him, take him back where he came from. Most of our close friends were church people, counselors and therapists, and no one knew what to do. We gave Charles a lot of attention but he wanted his brother gone. As they got older, James accommodated and attempted to please Charles any way he could. Later in life, he told Charles "You were a first-class bastard to me growing up." He was.

Charles was also a bed wetter until he was nine or ten, and this added to his problems.

John and Pat Caron lived across the street from us. They had two girls and we had two boys the same ages. We often talked about which gender was harder to raise, and sometimes we even talked about swapping kids. John was well known in the city of Haverhill as a decorated war veteran. He had been a prisoner for four years and twice allowed himself to be a decoy so that some of his buddies escaped. Two subsequent times he was used as a decoy without his consent. He had made one vow to himself. If he survived the war he would have ice cream every day for the rest of his life. And so he did.

He and I were both avid fishermen and we had taken a trip to New Hampshire with poles and rods. We were planning another trip when John suddenly developed polio and died. The community was in shock. Pat asked me to speak at John's funeral and was upset to learn that the Catholic church would not allow a Protestant clergyman to participate. I could be a pallbearer but that was it.

Pat was unprepared for such a tragedy in many ways. Their assets were all in John's name and therefore untouchable until the estate was settled. We loaned her money for weeks just so she could buy groceries.

The Catholic church was at the height of a campaign to develop separate, competing organizations in every aspect of life: Catholic schools, Catholic Boy Scout troops, Catholic Girl Scout troops. The policy was obviously one of non-fraternization with non-Catholics and it would not bode well for the future of Catholicism. It created two kinds of Catholics. One I called ignorant Catholics—unquestioning people who allowed the church to tell them what to do. The other group was better-educated and more independent in thought. Most of my neighbors were in the second group.

I was still enrolled as a graduate student, working on a thesis for my Ph.D. My goal was to study the religious caste system in America. I proposed studying the effects of a mixed marriage between Protestants and Catholics, which doesn't sound like a big deal today but, in those days, it was an important subject. I studied 25 marriages in which both were Protestant, 25 in which both were Catholic and 25 that identified as mixed. I found that if the marriage was taking place in a predominately Catholic neighborhood, both eventually became Catholic, and the same was true of the marriages in Protestant neighborhoods. More of the children were baptized and in church schools.

The mixed marriages suffered much more conflict over religious affiliation. If the marriage was strong, the couple tended to maintain religious training and the children attended church school. I thought it was significant that eleven of the children in the mixed marriages had not been baptized and were not receiving religious training.

I was beginning to do more counseling and receiving ever more satisfaction from helping people through their problems. But learning goes both ways, and I had an experience early on that helped shape my ministry. A fellow minister in a neighboring Methodist church referred a couple to me for marriage counseling. They had knocked on his door and said they wanted to be married that night. The minister could not do it without counseling them first and he would be on vacation. "Are you able to do it?" he asked. I said I would and he gave them directions to my house.

An hour later they arrived with two children, a boy five and a girl four, who looked neglected. On hearing their story, I thought the couple had little in their favor and I made a quick judgment that they could not possibly have a successful marriage. They had both been married before and the children were from her marriage. She had recently been given custody of them after they had spent the previous year in a foster home.

She was neatly dressed and from a middle-class family who were not at all happy with her. Though she had a master's degree, she had trouble holding a job. The man came from a large family—the tenth child of parents who were exhausted and overburdened. As a child, he was on his own and had fended for himself. He was a high school dropout and now a truck driver for a large construction company. He had met the woman at church and they had known each other for only three months.

I told them it was simply not possible for me to marry them that evening. First of all, I required a series of counseling sessions and, secondly, I needed to be convinced their marriage would be successful. I was not sure I could be convinced. The man said, "Tell us what you want us to do. We are going to get married and we want you to marry us."

For six months I met with them weekly and I found them to be one of the most delightful couples I had ever worked with. He had a drinking problem he needed to face. They agreed she would handle the finances and he would have five dollars a month to spend on beer. The need for the beer disappeared as the relationship developed. He returned to school to earn his high school diploma. After six months I was convinced it could work and I married them.

As they were leaving, the man said, "You have put us through a tough course. We'll be coming back on the Sunday of our anniversary and report to you." They lived 50 miles away but made the trip for the next ten years and shared their stories of joy and survival. Their son was in an accident in which his legs were so badly burned they were going to be amputated. A skin graft specialist became aware of the story, offered his services and saved the boy's legs. At the tenth visit, I learned that their son was the star basketball player at the school.

Ever after, I was cautious about making quick judgments. They were inspiring, willing to work for their marriage, and offered me hope.

All in all, Bradford helped me to admit a more diverse group of people into my sphere. I was in two worlds—serving a blue-collar church of ordinary, decent, hard-working folks, and associating with the outstanding businessmen in the community as a member of the Kiwanis Club. Being with this group, working with them, even counseling them with drinking problems helped me to modify my bias against the business community. I was becoming less uninitiated and a lot more savvy about people.

I was always grateful for Fay Gemmell, my fellow friend and minister, just up the road in Lawrence. We met often and talked about the ministry and where we were going and what we wanted and, yes, whether we were good Methodists. We had begun questioning ourselves in exactly the same way, which led to many rich conversations. We felt we were not as successful as traditional ministers.

And we asked: What is the purpose of my life and ministry? What mission should motivate me? In the thinking of our bishops, the mission of the minister was to convert. The authority to convert was based on an assumption of superiority, of being right. We thought we knew how to love people but we were not good at converting people.

We believed that our role was to seek and speak to the best in people so the best would come out. We felt that we were working on a new frontier because of our training in counseling. Our growing skills in counseling separated us from our fellow ministers. It wasn't that long ago when counseling skills were not thought to be useful tools for ministers. We knew they were—we were seeing results. Both Fay and I seemed to be going in a different direction from our bishops and we did not know where this soul searching would lead. Thank God, I had such a friend to go with me on this journey.

Though my experience in Bradford increased my growth and self-confidence, it did not prepare me for what was coming next.

1) The Old Stone Tavern, built in 1788 with walls two feet thick, was for a while the home of the man for whom the town had been named 11 years earlier, Clement Moore. Today it's part of the spruced-up Historic District.

2) Street scene in downtown Moorefield in the 1880's.

3) The Taylor building in downtown Moorefield, circa 1875, has been home to everything from the weekly newspaper, the Courier and Advertiser in the 19th century, to Friddle's barbershop, a fixture for 60 years, in the 20th.

4) The home and office of Dr. O. V. Brooks, our family physician, right next door to the Taylor building on North Main Street; his son taught me how to swim.

5) The Busy Bee Restaurant and pool hall where our local policeman, Mr. Robinette, confronted the Shoemaker gang.

6) My dad, Orvon Ray Bean, in his WW1 uniform.

7) (L to R): My grandparents Mahlon and Mary (Brown) Bean with Mary's nephew, Charles Brown and Mahlon's sister, Virginia Bean.

8) My mom Essye's grandfather, Godfrey Reed.

9) Still more Beans on top of Simon Bean Mountain.

10) My high school yearbook picture, 1940.

11) The Moorefield High School Glee Club, 1940; that's me, president, at the piano with (seated) left to right, Emma Heltzel, Jean Leatherman, Helen See, Jean Smith, Lorean Poland and Lura Hardy and (standing) Muriel Kessel, Jean Snider, Genevieve Runions, June Compton, Elda Leatherman, Gladys Barr, Mary Woerner, Helen Bowman, Zella Halterman, Carlton Saville, Lola Halterman, Paul Elosser, Flossie Zirk, Wayne Kessel, Weldon Neff, Mary Harman, Andy MacCorcle, Anne Williams, Mary Elder Inskeep, Vera Sions, Burnell Kessel, Naomi Taylor, Marguerite Herbaugh and Dorothy Fitzwater.

12) My brother Charles, who perished in WW II; he still holds, I do believe, the football scoring record at Moorefield High.

13) My brother Rodney in uniform; he was drafted by the Navy in 1945, his senior year in high school.

14) The post office in downtown Moorefield where I saw Christine for the first time.

15) Chris and I strolling in Washington D.C.

16) Among the blossoms at Boston Public Garden, 1946.

17) Chris and I during my first ministry at Peabody Methodist Church.

18) (L to R) The Hubers, the Lieders and the Beans
on winter vacation in New Hampshire.

19) Chris with our first-born, Charlie; that's our house in Peabody on the right.

20) Chris holding a friend's baby during my ministry at Bradford Methodist.

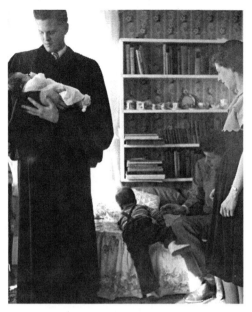

21) Our ministerial friend, Walter Nyberg, holding our second-born, Jim, after baptizing him, while older brother Charlie rough-houses on the couch.

22) Our friends Craig Lindell (upper left), his brother Carl sitting next to him with arms folded, and Billy Reed (up on top) along with two other fellow hikers.

23) I was never so proud as the day when Ennis Bowie, the first New Bedford Rodman Job Corps graduate, received his certificate (from Dr. Morris Better, Curriculum Director); on the right is John Morris, Team Coordinator looking on. Ennis was immediately hired by IBM.

WALLEN BEAN
FOR DARTMOUTH SELECTMAN

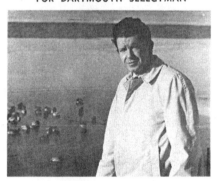

PLEDGES
PROGRESS

24) I spent $1500 and got 1500 votes; wasn't enough.

25) Chris in a rare moment away from the easel, 1995.

Chapter 12

West Roxbury

My next assignment was in West Roxbury, a suburb of Boston. At the time we had a beautiful, loving cat, in spite of Chris's allergies. Charles was seven and carrying our cat into the parsonage when a young neighbor greeted us. She was carrying her cat and said,

"Too bad you have a cat. My cat is a killer cat."

Within a week I heard a killer cat fight on our porch. I grabbed a broom and ran downstairs where I saw fur from one end of the porch to the other. The cat next door went slowly home. Both cats went to the vet, but the neighbor's cat did not return.

The personality of our cat changed. As a terrified tomcat, he began to challenge every cat in a wide area, coming home after battles, chewed up and sore from claw marks and punctures. This went on for almost a year before he did not return at all. In some crazy way, this episode was a foreshadowing of what would happen to me at the church.

At this time, West Roxbury Methodist Church was a sick church. By this, I mean it was ingrown, rigid, and did not want new members. It was secretive and closed and much gossip went on in the back rooms, over the telephone wires, and on Sunday mornings. I could see trouble soon after I arrived.

There were good people too, people who tried hard to restore health to the church. One such couple was Bruce and Pat Ward. Both were leaders and loyal Methodists; they verified the lack of friendliness and openness I found there. To prove a point, Bruce suggested that I study the names in the guest book for the past several years, and so I did. I was astounded to find the names of persons who had attended the church for as long as a year and left for other churches. Included was the daughter of one of the conference ministers and Jack Chase, the TV anchorman. (I later ministered to his family when his ten-year-old son fell out of an upstairs window and landed on his head, fracturing his skull.)

My appointment to this church was a turning point in my ministry. I was involved in one tangle or another the moment I arrived. The church actually had a proud history, but was being left behind by the rapid movement of people to the suburbs—this may have been the real source of its problems. Church members dug in and were defensive about everything.

First there was the problem of me getting my Ph.D. I was delighted to be only eight miles from Boston University so I could finish my dissertation. But when I voiced my intention, I was in immediate conflict with the lay leader and the official board. I had asked for one day a week as a legal requirement to return to BU to do my research and also teach an evening course on Marriage and Family under Dr. John Green. They would have none of it.

The church had sustained a great loss with the sudden death of their last young pastor after he had finished his Ph.D. He had left a pregnant wife, a year-old child and many sad parishioners. But the story was bigger than this. My predecessor had indeed gone back to school to finish his Ph.D. and then had accepted a coveted position on a national magazine. This proud church had suffered a loss in status, thinking they were a training ground for student ministers, a second-class church.

He also tried to make changes in the governance and this did not go over well. He had used a clause in the Methodist discipline to limit the terms of the trustees and ushers; they could not succeed themselves after two terms. Some trustees and ushers had held their positions for over twenty years. They were now out of their jobs and not happy. So they were not happy with me.

My first run-in was with the head usher—ushers are elected by the congregation and have a lot of power. A young man had been attending services with a child of kindergarten age and was leaving during the singing of the last hymn. I wanted to reach out and perhaps get the child into Sunday school—we had only four children in the kindergarten class. So I asked the usher for the man's name and he said he did not know. I asked the next week and the next. He said he had asked the man some months ago and was too embarrassed to ask again. Of course, the young man disappeared. No attempt was made to increase membership and get a more diverse congregation.

Everything I planned or tried to bring about became a clash with the lay leader. I thought of having a series of prayer study groups that would meet in the homes of parishioners. It was shot down by the lay leader with the comment that if any praying was to take place, the minister was the one being paid to do it. Incredibly, it was thought I was trying to get out of doing my job.

So many problems ensued, it's hard to list them all. The church was in debt and really struggling. I began to visit nearby trailer camps and new apartment buildings to welcome people to the church. An increase in attendance would also mean an increase in financial support. Quite a few of my recruits were interns employed in the many area hospitals. I made the effort to visit people in 24 hospitals during my four years there. But change was not welcomed.

The church members were proud of their long record of attendance but it was a closed society. A highlight of the year was the celebration of membership Sunday in which the oldest members were feted. New ones need not apply.

The list goes on. The choir had five members and a paid soloist who had sung together for 20 years. I recruited ten young adults to join the choir and what happened? The five permanent members quit. The organist who had played for over 30 years, a well-known Christian Scientist, died while I was pastor and not a single member of the congregation was invited to the private funeral service. I am guessing she still did not feel welcome after decades of playing there.

The condition of the church basement caused more problems. Janitors in the past had piled ashes against the studs holding up the stairs causing them to nearly crash. The lay leader of the church, a dictator, would not even discuss the problem. Fittingly, God intervened. An Irish carpenter joined the church and he brought his crowbar and banged at the basement floor to see what was underneath. He found a concrete drain under the church. Hurricane Carol flooded the Episcopal Church down the street but left our building dry. Something good happened.

And did I say our third son, John, was born while we were in West Roxbury? A tumultuous time for a young innocent to arrive on the scene.

Chapter 13

Rolling Ridge

The New England Conference of the Methodist Church ran a retreat in North Andover, MA at Rolling Ridge, a perfect place to experience the power of small groups. I truly believed that one week at the conference center had a more profound impact and developed more intense relationships than a year of church going. Rolling Ridge most certainly served its purpose as a place for reflection and inquiry. Originally the land was a summer retreat for a multimillionaire from Chicago, but it became so much more when the Methodist church bought it for $50,000—28 acres of landscaped trees and forest on a lakeshore. The building complex was in top condition and could house 120 people. The landscape was highlighted by a corridor of rhododendrons about 40 feet long leading to the edge of the lake where a fountain shot a stream of water 60 feet in the air. It was a wonderful place to get married.

For twenty years, Christine and I had served on the staff for a week at a time. Some weekends were exclusively for young adults and many came from my church. One weekend the kids had a lively debate over who could drink safely. They decided that immature individuals or teenagers could not; also, those who were grieving, or under stress, or carried too much anger. The program included a lot of old-fashioned hymn singing, which the kids loved. Ten young people from this group decided to join the choir, but the present choir took it as criticism and they all quit.

One of the most popular staff members was a tall, lanky Scot named James Laird, my predecessor at Peabody, the inspirational leader of the conferences for high school young people. He was eventually appointed as pastor of the First Methodist Church of Detroit and his congregation included CEOs and labor unions of the auto industry. A very big deal and a close friend.

Hurricane Carol hit the summer we were at Rolling Ridge, and that's not all that happened. We had 125 high school-age young people at the Ridge for a full week and our stint began with one disaster after another. First the Center director fell and broke his arm, followed by more misery: the grounds superintendent suffered a serious injury that put him out of commission for the week. Next a staff member had an attack of appendicitis and had to return home for surgery. My land cruiser Oldsmobile was the fastest car at the Center and I was asked to take him to Athol. When I started the car, it caught on fire. Everyone pitched in by the shovelful from a nearby sand pile and put the fire out.

Then on Wednesday, Hurricane Carol hit with 95-mile-an-hour winds. We were completely unprepared because the weather forecast said the storm had slowed and would turn into a nor'easter. At the height of the storm, two students decided they wanted to see what it would be like out in the woods in a hurricane. I saw them and called them back; the force of the wind, 90 miles per hour, threw the sound back in my face. I ran to get them with trees falling dangerously around me. We did not have any electricity for the rest of the week.

We survived but lost forty 200-year-old pine, oak and maple trees from the landscaped estate. The line of rhododendrons that formed the stately corridor leading to the water fountain miraculously escaped damage. But the place was a mess and it was impossible to imagine the storybook place it was just a week ago.

It was not all hurricanes and hard times at Rolling Ridge. One evening after a rather quiet meditation program, Jim Laird was in charge of the heavy-duty discussion. When it was time to take a break, he asked if one of the young people had a song he or she would like to teach the group. A student said she had one but it came out of kindergarten and required a set of motions to go along with the song. This is how it goes:

> In a cottage in a wood
> Little man by a window stood
> Saw a rabbit passing by
> Knocking at the door.
> Help me, help, the rabbit said,
> Before the hunter shoots me dead

Little rabbit come inside
Safely there you will abide.

The song is repeated six times with actions. The first line, you make a square with your hands, the second line, a salute, the third a hopping action with two fingers, the fourth you knock. On the fifth, you lift both arms, the sixth, you aim a gun, the seventh, you motion 'come in', and the eighth, you pet the back of your hand. As the song becomes faster, it is impossible to do the actions. Halfway through the scene, Jim gyrates around flinging his arms, wildly out of control. A couple of staff slipped off to the kitchen, put on long aprons, grab Jim by his hands, lift him up and carry him into the kitchen. The group went into hysterics. That kindergarten stuff works for the big kids too.

As it happened, I taught this little ditty to the Kiwanis Club in Haverhill. It produced gales of laughter and was passed on by other Kiwanis Clubs across the country until a member of the Haverhill Club was in California and heard it sung while attending a meeting there.

Ah, those days of innocence. Where did they go?

This was not an innocent time for the Methodist Church. It was the fifties and the anti-communist crusade was in full swing. My friend Jim Laird had been appointed to the First Methodist Church in Detroit, and he became a follower of a famous preacher in Detroit, Henry Hitt Crane, one of the most influential American Methodist ministers of the twentieth century. He was a fervent pacifist, a supporter of racial equality, civil liberties and workers' rights. The Methodist church was very much involved in social justice. Hence, the church was under attack and so was Jim Laird.

Stanley High, a reporter, had written an article entitled "The Pink Fringe" that appeared in The Reader's Digest. In it, he attacked the clergy of the Methodist Church calling it anti-American and pro-communist. Clare Boothe Luce, the editor, was in turn attacked for publishing the story and she denied any responsibility, claiming there was no editorial policy to add fire to the anti-communist crusade. Henry thought otherwise and had it out with the magazine, withdrawing a story he had written for them. At the time, Reader's Digest altered personal account stories to make them fit a policy requiring four elements for each story: sex, personal, communist threat and God.

Henry told a story to illustrate the hidden policies of Readers Digest: *A writer came to the editor's office with a story he said they would like. The editor asked him for the title. "How to Seduce a Bear," the man replied. And the editor said, "We like that. It's very catchy. But how can we make it more personal?" The writer replied, "How I Seduced a Bear." The editor asked, "How can we incorporate the country's political agenda?" The writer offered, "How I Seduced a Bear for the FBI." And then the editor wondered about adding a religious element to it because there was a lot of religious fervor at the time. And the title became: "How I Seduced a Bear for the FBI and Found God."*

We sometimes forget what a frightening time it was in America. Freedom of thought and speech were being systematically killed off. Innocent citizens were under suspicion and afraid of saying the wrong thing, lest they be accused of being traitors. It was especially hard for ministers, teachers, actors, anyone who worked in the public sphere. You had to watch your backside, watch your mouth, edit yourself. I continued just being myself and eventually this ruthless crusade managed to kill itself. The Methodist church survived, as did the clergy.

Henry Hitt Crane's most famous saying was: *"Each of us should do something everyday that we do not want to do but we know we should do. To strengthen our backbone. And put iron in our soul."*

Wicked stuff.

At church, we had almost enough young adults to make two solid youth groups, but the groups were vastly different. One consisted of kids who were stable keepers of the rules; they were good students, did not use drugs and were the pride of the church. The other group were rebels at home and at church. One of the rebel girls became pregnant and many adults in the church ostracized her. I remember the president of the women's society saying she felt like pulling her skirt aside to keep from contaminating herself every time she met this teenager in church. As minister, I was drawn more to the rebel group, as they clearly needed me more. I was told, however, that I had been hired to work with the "nice" group.

I could not get it right with this church.

There were happy times too at West Roxbury and they are part of the record. Our third son, John Douglas Bean, was born and he filled our lives with happiness. I did much fishing, climbing and hiking. Bruce Ward, one of my favorite congregants, was the director of the local YMCA and he loved challenges. One such challenge that drew local headlines was the trip he organized for 30 boys who traveled up the newly opened Alaskan highway. I didn't go on this one, but some of the boys from church did. What an eye-opener for them.

He also organized canoe trips to the Allagash Maine wilderness, a trip that takes two weeks. On the first trip, we saw lumbermen from the paper company marking mature trees to be harvested and they did careful cutting. On the last trip, we could see that the paper companies had a new strategy. They took everything, leaving a thin strip of mature trees to reseed the bare ground. Treeless areas silted the rivers and streams. Our beautiful wilderness was being invaded by chain saws, snowmobiles, even drunks and airplanes.

On one trip we were in the deep, deep woods and had to carry our canoes and supplies from one lake to the next, not an easy task. One night we arrived at the designated area to find a party already there, and they were boozing it up. Where did all that beer come from? We wondered. It would have been impossible to carry it such a distance in such quantities. The next morning we had our answer. A light plane landed and took off with the party. A plane actually swooped down into the wilderness and plucked the boozers out.

On another occasion, Chris and I were visiting the Gemmells in Keene, New Hampshire after a heavy snowfall. Mrs. Carl Smith, the wife of the Egyptian zoologist, the discoverer of King Tut's tomb, lived nearby. She had come down the hill to get the mail. Their house was guarded with the most up-to-date equipment and signs warned that you must go through security checks, as it was full of King Tut materials. Suddenly she was in a panic when a snowmobile flew up the hill, bypassing security. With increased access, nothing in the wilderness was safe anymore.

All in all, I felt the church was unhappy with my work—they would have been unhappy with any minister's work. I tried but could not change the culture of the church, and I did not ever want to be in such a situation again. The annual Methodist Conference was coming up and I would be appointed to a new church. I made up my mind that I would not go into an unhappy situation again. I would not serve a church that had such profound problems or doubts about me and the way I ministered, including my deep interest in counseling.

I called my friend, Emerson Smith, who had a special appointment as chaplain to labor and business. I told him of my constant conflicts within the church and my fear of ending up in the same situation again. Among other things, he had knowledge of the bishop's thinking and said the bishop was fearful that if I completed my doctorate, I would be leaving the parish ministry to either teach or accept a counseling job, and he wanted me as far away from Boston University as I could get.

This was ridiculous, but it was not the first time I had a confrontation with the bishop. The other was worse. He had called a special session to discuss the illness of five young men from parsonage families. He said he believed there was not enough Bible reading and praying going on in those families and that's why they were ill. I spoke up and said there were other causes that created problems for parsonage children. I offered a litany of reasons, then mentioned that my wife had married me in spite of the fact that I was going to be a minister—she never wanted to be a minister's wife.

The bishop was astonished. He said, "You mean you have been married all these years and you have not converted her yet?" I couldn't believe what he was saying and, for the first time, I could see the problem clearly. My passion for counseling had become a threat to his authority. To him, the role of the minister was to convert and, over the years, I had less and less interest in converting. Counseling is a different skill. It relies on active and disciplined listening and exploring options—its goal is growth. This is where my heart was going.

The events of that Conference set the stage for some major changes in my life. A friend who was to be appointed the next superintendent in Athol paid me a visit and asked if he could send a pastoral committee to my Sunday service. Would I accept his parish once he was appointed? I was pleased with his offer and that same day I told my own superintendent of the conversation. He huffed and puffed—no one had called him. He said under no circumstances would he recommend me for the Athol church.

I did not know at that time I was also being considered for the job as chaplain at Deaconess Hospital. Also, I began to receive inquiries from churches outside the conference, one in Lebanon, New Hampshire and the other in Orleans on Cape Cod. Before the day was over, I had decided to become pastor of the Orleans Methodist Church and transfer from the New England Conference to the New England Southern Conference.

I guess I had joined the rebel group.

Chapter 14

Orleans (1957-1962)

Cape Cod is a sand bar extending into the Atlantic ocean, 75 miles from the canal to Provincetown. The town of Orleans is located on the inner elbow of the Cape and is dotted with bogs, ponds, inlets, islands and harbors, a place of beauty, especially for fishermen.

Nevertheless, I expected our move to Orleans would be a low point in my ministry. We were moving to a new conference and leaving behind established relationships. Christine had her hands full with three active boys and a largely absentee husband. A minister's wife is among the most demanding roles a woman could take on—a high percentage of marriages fail because the minister is too busy consoling others. So when we arrived, I did not have a lot of confidence. My career felt shaky, my marriage felt shaky. I didn't know if we had made the right move.

The Orleans Church was viewed by some of my colleagues as Siberia and the community was called "The Sick Sandbar." Its pathology was greater than parts of the South End in Boston. In those days, Cape Cod was not the quaint, fancy vacation place it is today. It was quaint, yes, but also poor, isolated, and riddled with social problems.

The Cape family was dominated by the tides. Tides determined when one went to church, when one saw the doctor, or when one could go to children's birthday parties. The Cape Cod woman had a reputation. She managed the family budget, made most family decisions, and therefore was dominant. It was said that the typical Cape boy would begin fishing early, drop out of school at 16, work like a Trojan, never read a book and never get a new idea.

The typical Cape girl would graduate from high school, marry at 18, have two children by age 20, then a lover, and finally a hysterectomy by age 30. It was amazing how frequently doctors gave this advice: women should have hysterectomies in order to prevent problems later.

My church, thank the Lord, was a happy place. Here in Orleans, we moved into the smallest of all the parsonages we'd lived in. The church was also small—it had 40 members. The building itself was beautiful and carried a $40,000 mortgage, the result of a recent renovation. One parishioner made a spectacular contribution. He purchased an old Cape Cod home that had belonged to a sea captain and found a barn full of antiques. Among the items were dozens of crystals and he had a chandelier made for the church as part of his gift to the building fund.

And here is a testament to that church in Siberia. The parishioners put on ten suppers during the summer and invited the public. They fed 200 people at each supper and retired the mortgage during the four years I served the church. I had the best time of my ministry in Orleans.

The discovery of Cape Cod as a vacation spot was just beginning; the population of Orleans when I arrived was about 2200. Orleans was a Republican town—only ten people were registered as Democrats. Christine felt that she should help even the score and registered as a Democrat. She was enlisted as a poll watcher during elections while I earned the title of the husband of "that Democratic woman."

The popularity of the Cape exploded during the four years we lived there. The towns were isolated enclaves and fishing was the primary source of work. The fishing families were close and many were uncomfortable going off the Cape or, for that matter, more than ten miles from their homes. My first efforts to organize a Council of Churches failed for that reason. Years later, when I was working in another capacity, we succeeded in forming such a Council.

In one of those flukes of life, I became a public person perhaps sooner than I would have liked. I began teaching a course at BU on Marriage Preparation and a reporter got wind of it and asked for an interview. A full-page article appeared in The Cape Cod Standard-Times and I became known almost instantly. It referred to me as a successful marriage counselor and the piece was entitled "Romeo and Juliet didn't have a Chance." I had discussed the Marriage Prediction Schedules used to evaluate a couple's potential for success, and they picked up on Romeo as a "cute" title. Well, it got people's attention and the flood of requests began.

Besides this publicity, a Falmouth lawyer, who was married to an old classmate of mine from West Virginia, began to refer his friends to me—apparently I was one of the few resources on the Cape for people experiencing marital problems. Or any problems, for that matter. Several psychiatrists and psychologists lived on the upper Cape but they all practiced in Boston. And in nearby New Bedford, there was a two-year waiting list for services for children.

The Orleans church supported me in my growing role as a counselor and eventually a parishioner was giving me 20 hours a week of secretarial help. Her husband was asked if he and Louise were having trouble. When he said no, he replied, "Well, she sure is spending a lot of time in that counseling minister's office."

Along with the pleasant atmosphere in the church, I found much joy in nature. Orleans was a fisherman's paradise and, as you know by now, fishing was my great love. Many varieties of both fresh and salt-water fish thrived in nearby ponds and the ocean. We lived on fish, or so it seemed to the boys. Clams were everywhere too. We ate small, hard shell clams called freestones, raw on the half shell; larger clams, either sea clams or quahogs, were the main ingredients in chowder. Littlenecks ended up as fried clams.

Fresh water trout swam in the ponds, stocked by the state, and a trout hatchery was located in Bourne. Smallmouth black bass and largemouth bass were plentiful. A largemouth bass could swallow a baitfish half its size. When I was using a seine to catch small fish for bait, I caught a largemouth bass.

Every avid fisherman looks for the magic touch that will bring fish to you, the sure thing. I read somewhere that the odor of sugar was pleasant to trout and salmon. Marshmallows were a treat too, but bourbon was at the top of the list, so the rumor went.

I told my friend Colonel Crapo (rhymes with 'maypole', sort of) what I'd learned just before we made plans to fish Peter's Pond. We were going in his boat and he went through an elaborate ritual preparing things just so when suddenly he stopped, picked up a mustard jar and said, "You see, this is bourbon. You have told me so many outlandish fish stories, I never know whether to believe you, but this tale about bourbon has promise."

We anchored in his favorite spot near the sand pit. The colonel was using corn for bait. He dipped the corn in the bourbon and let out his line. I was using worms dug from my compost. Before I could get my slow worm on the bottom, he had a trout in the boat. He landed his limit of five trout before I had a hit. Bourbon, would you believe it? Of course, it didn't work for me but then I don't drink bourbon!

Remember this: If a Methodist preacher is caught smoking a stogie, eating marshmallows and drinking bourbon, there is good scientific reason for it.

But the fish stories don't end there. My friend from graduate school, Martin Cook, loved fishing and came to the Cape to join me in an adventure or two. In the Seminary Singers, he was a soloist with a beautiful baritone voice. Martin was an incredibly disciplined student and for two years did nothing but research his thesis, then sat down at the typewriter, wrote his dissertation and had it accepted with very little change. He had served a Methodist Church on the Cape as a student but had never landed a big striped bass. On this occasion he arrived with his double-hulled aluminum boat with a 35-horsepower motor all the way from Lake Erie.

We had planned to leave at 5 a.m. and meet up with the big bass as they were feeding at the turning of the tide. Marvin was late getting his several rods together but the water was as smooth as silk. Then as the waves came I hooked a large bass on the first cast. Marvin could not get even one cast until we had landed the one I had hooked. By then, the school had stopped feeding and Marvin was fit to be tied.

That evening we went again. The wind had started blowing about five miles an hour, a warning to me that the calm weather was about to change. I told Martin we could not stay long, that we'd go again next morning, but he wanted to linger until the turning of the tide.

"We must remain in the channel," I said. No sooner had I said the words when he cast with the small rod, a 12-pound test line, and hooked a huge fish. Against my better judgment, I headed into the breakers and followed the fish until we were outside in calmer water. For the next hour Marvin played the fish in the open water until, finally exhausted, it turned over on its side. While Marvin held the line taut, I slid the gaff under its gills and lifted it into the boat. Marvin let out a yell of exaltation at its size.

My only concern was how to get back to shore. It was not yet dark so I followed a lobster fisherman and we got in safely. At the tackle store, he weighed his fish and it was 44 pounds. The store verified the line on which it was caught and the details were submitted to "Field and Stream" magazine. Marvin had his record—he had come east for just that reason. You would think he would be satisfied but he just had to go back on the outgoing tide. The weather report called for showers later in the day and

I told him I'd go but we would have to stay inside the channel for safety reasons. "And use the lighter rod and smaller plugs," I advised.

In passing the Chatham Light there was no small craft warning flag up. The earlier fog had lifted and I glimpsed cloudbanks in the east but my attention was focused on fish. Suddenly the fog came straight down and disoriented us. It was 9 a.m. and we waited for it to lift. An ominous breeze stirred the water and I ran the boat up and down Monomoy Island looking for a break in the thick fog. The wind increased. I felt panic, and then heard the sound of a motor. Moving toward it, I came upon the channel marker and decided it was a logical place to tie up and wait. Nearby I could hear someone pulling his pots and a man called over asking me if I was in trouble.

"Yup. Where's the channel?"

"Set your compass due west and you'll get there."

I headed west and ran into sand bars. We could hear the roar of the big breakers and that was not reassuring. The tide had turned and soon the sand bars would be underwater. We were running out of gasoline, the wind had become a gale, and the fog was thick as pea soup

"Is your boat insured?" I asked Martin.

"Yes."

"Then we're going to pick the biggest wave and ride it ashore. When we hit, get out as fast as you can as the waves are high enough to knock us out."

"The boat will float because of its double hull," he shouted.

"No, it will quickly fill with sand and water."

He was close to panic when we ran ashore on Monomoy. The impact popped his tackle box open and filled the boat with fishing plugs. Thinking the anchor would save the boat, he pulled on the anchor rope and a hook snagged the joint of his finger and the rope. I took out my trusty Barlow pocketknife and cut the rope. Up the sand dune he scrambled while I removed the motor from the boat.

We walked the quarter mile to the mainland and went straight to the doctor's office. This we learned: a storm off the Jersey coast had generated the 50 mile-an-hour winds and the beach patrol missed us when they went inland to check a cottage. Around 4 p.m. we returned to the spot where we'd beached the boat and all we found was a twisted pile of aluminum.

There were two businesses in Orleans that catered to the needs of fishermen: Mac Reed's Bait Shop and The Hummock. Mac sold eels, night crawlers, minnows, grass shrimp and the less expensive fishing equipment and weather gear. He also took people on fishing trips, providing a boat and acting as guide. Almost every day he ate fish, mostly trout, and cooked it in a frying pan right in the shop. We became friends while I was pastor and built a lifelong friendship around fishing.

Mac had an apartment over the bait shop and, after I left the Cape, I slept over when I returned to fish. He always had a large tin full of the best muffins on the Cape. When he grew old, his daughter Pat assumed the management of the store, but all I had to do was walk in and he was ready to go. He was 90 by then. After his wife died, he developed a friendship with a woman who had buried three husbands. They went on trips, were active in my church and he made thousands of his muffins for church suppers.

After Mac's death I continued to make his shop my Cape home. In her way, Pat took Mac's place and whenever I walked into the shop she was ready to close up and go fishing. She made one request of me. Since I was now working in New Bedford, a garment and leather-manufacturing city, she asked for a large leather pocketbook with four deep pockets. She wanted to use one of the pockets to hold eels (used as bait to catch large bass). I looked everywhere and never found a pocketbook that would quite work for a fisherwoman. The designers simply lacked the imagination.

Goose Hummock was the store for the elite, owned by Governor Francis Sargent who was an avid fisherman. In those days, trout fishing was illegal until the opening of the season in April. Hundreds of trout were stocked and every fisherman had his favorite pond to fish in that first day. Governor Sargent had chosen to fish in Crystal Pond. I was talking with Freddie McFarland, manager of the store, saying I'll bet there would be extra big trout in the governor's pond.

"If you have complaints, tell HIM," said Freddie. The governor was standing behind me with a smile on his face. I learned later that he caught the largest trout in Crystal Pond.

In those days, the lower Cape was a wilderness. Thousands of bird species lived on Cape Cod or used it as a resting station in their flight from southern destinations to northern nesting grounds. The glacial potholes left by the accumulation of debris when the glacial ice melted were teeming with fish and other forms of aquatic animals.

That first summer, we had a house full of company, and our well went dry. I called a trustee who said, "Well, call the plumbers." I called the Smith Brothers who said they would come on Monday and drive a point. Water could be had by driving a point into the sand about 20 feet.

I became acutely aware for the first time that the Cape was a true sand bar and that the only fresh water that fed over 250 lakes and ponds was rainwater. Its presence produced enough pressure to keep the sea water out. Such water accumulated in the sand and we supplied our wells. Thus the most expensive land was the literal seashore.

I waited a week for the plumbers to come and spent a good part of the day carrying water from my neighbor's house. I finally called another trustee who informed me that Smith Brothers might make promises, but the only way to really get a plumber was to be at their office first thing Monday morning and get the first plumber who came in. It worked. Two men came to the house and it took them a week to drive the point. One was a young man who was concerned that we had waited two weeks for water while entertaining friends.

During the week the well was drilled, we got well acquainted with the plumber and our neighbor too, Mrs. Hildreth Putnam. The following summer she lost her water and the same two men came to drill her well. The young plumber, who was now active in the church, asked if he could hook up a garden hose from the outside faucet of the parsonage to our neighbor's house so she could have water.

"WHAT?" I exclaimed. "We could have done that last summer!"

He was so embarrassed, he never said no to any request I made of him including asking him to become an adviser to a church youth group.

Almost overnight, visitors began falling in love with the Cape and the permanent population swelled. Many impulsively quit their jobs, sold their homes and moved to Cape Cod, not realizing the Cape economy was tied to a summer season of four months. The one activity that now continued year-round was building and many of the newcomers became carpenters.

Our church population began growing. A dozen teenagers showed up on Sunday morning interested in forming a youth group. I knew I would need some help, and Frank and Ruth Ireland became the advisers. The group quickly grew to 20 members and group dynamics became more complicated. When three young men were not sure they were accepted, they moved out of the circle and became hecklers by opposing anything the advisers suggested. Ruth was upset when the outsiders led the group to boycott the singing of Christmas carols. She decided to finish the year but would not be an adviser next year.

The group met after Christmas and learned too late that Ruth was unhappy. After several meetings, they gathered around the piano and sang Christmas carols, trying to make up. Before the year was over, the group had grown to 30 kids with no adviser at all. They approached Frank and Ruth several more times and they agreed to consider it under two conditions: Since there were now 40 in the group, it needed at least two couple advisers. They also wanted the young people to draw leaders from the group and let them play a leading role.

But Frank suffered from a much bigger problem than that of the youth group. He was an alcoholic. He had inherited a good business, a tire re-treading plant, and it was hard to manage the business with a drinking problem. His five brothers and sisters received separate settlements, but his mother was to have her bills paid by the business. She had left the community and probably did not know Frank was in financial trouble. He stopped drinking with the help of AA and a special friend. But he still lost his business, and it was a sad day when I stood on the front porch of his home and his house was auctioned off.

Life in the neighborhood was good for kids. When Jim turned eight in January (we had been there eight months), we planned a birthday party as a way of introducing him to potential friends. A telephone call came an hour before the party.

"Can we bring Jim a puppy as a birthday gift?" one of the kids asked. At first, Christine said no, then she thought of the dilemma for the boy and called back and said yes. This is how Cindy came into our lives.

She was the runt of a litter that grew up to look like Labrador Retrievers with short hair and massive heads. But Cindy was half the size of the rest of the litter, had long hair and an energy level hard to control. She had a need to run. When she got loose, she would be gone for hours and return home smelling of dead fish in the hot sun and anything else she could roll around in. She needed a bath before she could be near anyone, let alone be in the house. She hated the bath and it was hard to catch her. She would bark in the middle of the night at anyone coming in the nearby Cove Motel. The next morning the police would call and say there were complaints. But she was a delight, and we decided to pay for obedience school for her and Jim, hoping some of the training would rub off on him.

Not until Orleans did Chris demand her night out, and she got it. She went to Provincetown once a week for a painting class. She never stopped studying in one class or another, with one artist or another. But I almost turned it into a disaster. I was babysitting the boys, working at a card table and using a bottle of ink. I fell asleep and Charles drank the entire bottle. I was in a panic and rushed him to the doctor's office. The doctor said it would not hurt him but he would have the stinkiest diapers and we would have to dispose of them.

"Your wife will be furious," he warned.

And so she was. I lost my reputation as a reliable babysitter.

In Orleans, I plunged into gardening, for better or worse. That first summer I found one blighted rhubarb plant and realized a previous occupant of the parsonage had a garden, and I decided I would have one too. I remembered reading about how the Indians grew corn, placing a herring in each hill of corn for fertilizer. What worked for corn would work for tomatoes. It was easy in those days to go to Brewster and seine a barrel of herring. Under each tomato, I carefully placed a herring.

We then left for two weeks vacation not knowing how much the numerous skunks in the neighborhood loved herring. The mischievous creatures dug out enough of the rotting herring to stink up the neighborhood. To be sure, I heard about it from the neighbors, but oh did those tomatoes love that "skunk ice cream." I fed the whole neighborhood, and they forgave me for the odorous price they paid.

Our favorite fish was flounder. In the fall they spawned in the freshwater pond nearby. We had purchased a freezer to preserve fish, scallops and clams. In the fall we'd buy a fish box with a glass bottom, put a bright light in the box, attach it to the side of a rowboat and, armed with a spear on a long pole, spear a fish. Sometimes we ended up with two hundred pounds for the freezer.

The second summer after the death of our neighbor, Mrs. Putnam, her son Edwin, who everybody called "Put," brought his wife Erleine and their family down from Brattleboro, Vermont to live in the house. We all instantly accepted each other and there was visible chemistry between Erleine and Christine. They were always laughing. They had three children too, almost the same ages as ours, and we seemed to become one family overnight.

I soon became aware that "Put" had a drinking problem, but I had learned not to let such troubles interfere with being a good neighbor. He would ask occasionally if I had seen a program on TV about alcohol. Our friendship led to some risky decisions on Chris' and my part. They were about to lose the land they had inherited on Route 6 in Eastham. It was a campground, their only property-producing income. Christine and I loaned Erleine $1700 for a year so they could make payments. "Put" may not have known about the loan; it was Erleine who was in charge.

In the fourth year of our friendship, when I had been transferred to a church in New Bedford, the family showed up in my office and "Put" said, "Tell me what I must do to stop drinking."

"Three things," I replied. "Make a commitment to yourself that you will stop drinking, join AA for two years, and find something to do for others to take the place of the huge block of time you have been spending at bars."

He joined AA for two years and never drank again.

That first year of sobriety his son Peter discovered an electric train in the basement and "Put" created a layout and formed a train club for the children in the neighborhood. Then he began to collect trains and repair them for others and he came to be known as the Trainman of the Cape. Now that he had stopped drinking, he developed the campground and ran a tight ship. He had been a Merchant Mariner for eight years and liked structure—he had rules and he expected them to be observed.

A neighbor's dog started visiting the campsites begging for food. "Put" got the owner's name and asked him to come get his dog. The next day the dog was back. This time "Put" called the animal officer and the dog was taken to the pound. It cost the owner $25 to get him back. I was visiting him when an angry man knocked on the door and asked for Mr. Putnam. "He's right there, coming up the lane," I said. He confronted "Put" who listened quietly as the man got angrier.

"What did he say?" Erleine asked, after the man left.

"Oh, he said I was a prick and I told him that may be so, but it doesn't solve the problem of the dog."

Perfect logic with a touch of wry. Anger is no match for cool.

Anyway, when "Put" was ready to sell his train collection, it was displayed at the campground and eventually sold. He never attended church but he was curious about what I said in my sermons. I remember him describing a version of The Good Samaritan story that illustrated the attitude of three different sorts of people.

The robbers said, "What is mine is mine and what is thine is mine if I can take it."

The busy travelers said, "What is mine is mine and what is thine is thine if you can keep it."

The Samaritan said, "What is mine is mine and what is mine is thine if you need it."

"Put" always wanted to know if his wife was included in this taking and giving.

There was one subject you could not tease him about. He did not think it funny at all when another Edwin H. Putnam moved into the village. Mail was mixed up. They were mixed up as couples. Their children were misidentified. Bank statements went to the wrong house. What a mess. He was right about this.

There was no trash collection on the Cape at this time—you hauled your own. The dump was a dried up pothole. As the population grew, so did the trash. The town hired a supervisor of the dump who determined where different items should be deposited and he made sure toxic materials were isolated. The dumps grew like Topsy and they became popular places to meet friends who had the same schedules. In the early days, before antiques became a craze, some treasure hunters picked carefully through dumps to find gold. The brother of my BU professor found a Ming dynasty vase that was worth several thousand dollars. Many Cape rental cottages were completely furnished by discarded furniture.

The dumps were overrun with rats. Some people bought boxes of 22 rifle short shells to see how many rats they could dispose of during the evening hours.

Ed Putnam – we didn't always call him "Put" - hauled his garbage to the dump in an old model T station wagon, which was usually loaded with trash from his campground. It had been painted. I was interested in antiques myself and I encouraged him to investigate what was underneath all that paint. Sure enough, he found tiger maple sidings, which showed it to be one of the first Ford station wagons and worth a lot of money.

He befriended an elderly lady one day by taking her shopping and doing odd jobs at her home. She asked him to take an old chair to the dump, and Erleine recognized it as a Queen Anne chair. When the elderly lady was informed of its value, she said it was of no value to her. It occupies a corner in the Putnam's living room to this day.

Erleine's interest in antiques led her to open a shop in their large garage, and she became a regular shopper in the growing number of yard sales.

One afternoon the siren at the fire station signaled, and we learned that two children were missing. The sound sent a chill through the men. They began a search for the little boys, three and five. They looked in the woods first and found nothing. I joined in the search with four members of our church but instead of going on a wild goose chase, we conferred to see if we could come up with a real plan. We were aware that the ice on the bogs had melted the day before and now it was bitterly cold. Was it possible they had fallen through the ice?

That's exactly where we found their little bodies, under the ice near their home. Their parents were devastated and the Catholic priest was called because the boys were enrolled in the new Catholic kindergarten. When he arrived, I decided to leave knowing that he would be in charge, but something incredible happened before I got out the door. The priest learned that the boys had never been baptized and therefore they could not have a Catholic funeral—that was that. So he said a prayer and left. I was appalled. I stayed until late that evening comforting the grieving parents and learning about the family. The mother, who had been married before, said her present husband was a Canadian Catholic who spoke only French.

They asked me to conduct the funeral. The mother said if it rained, she wanted the funeral canceled until the sun shone. The next morning, an enraged grandfather called and asked me to come to his home. A fundamentalist Baptist who had heard of the tragedy had been at their house for half an hour quoting scripture and implying that God was punishing the mother for her sins. I later learned that he was a known character in the town. He had created a scene at the local jail by insisting a prisoner had converted and given his life to God and therefore should be released. He had been banned from visiting the jail by the sheriff. I went to his church in Hyannis and told him that 20 miles was outside his parish and he was not to visit in mine. And so he stayed away.

After the funeral, the father of the boys insisted that I take a large sum of money to say prayers, which was his Catholic way of expressing his religious belief. This episode was one more experience in my education in the Catholic church.

And, yes, ministers do mess up. A church member asked if I would marry him and his fiancée. He had a large family with roots running back to the first settlements, but this would be a small affair due to the circumstances. His fiancée was a nurse, and it happened that she was the groom's brother's former wife. His brother had joined the army for four tours and seldom came home. When he finally decided to stay home, the couple realized they had not built a true marriage so they divorced and he resumed his career in the army.

Several weeks before the event, the couple asked me to marry them in a private ceremony, just the bride and groom, the best man and the mother-in-law. As I wrote down their names and the time of the wedding, they asked that their names be in code. I agreed but said my wife will know as she monitors my schedule. "Please put her name in code too," they requested.

The week of the wedding was a busy one for me. I spent most of it at the meeting of the annual Methodist Conference. When I returned I knew there were two important things I had to do. I had a commitment to speak at a baccalaureate service nearby. The other I could not remember. I was about to look it up in my date book when my wife said,

"Of course, it's Charles' piano recital."

Well, of course.

The couple looked for me all over the Cape when I did not show up at the church, assuming I had gone fishing. They had planned to go to the family birthday party for their 80-year-old grandfather after the wedding. They found another clergyman willing to perform the ceremony around 9 p.m. The next morning the mother-in-law called to ask whether I had missed an appointment the night before.

"Not that I can think of," I replied.

"You missed the wedding!"

I could have crawled through the nearest rat hole. I felt extreme mortification for weeks and months. I still do.

Environmental problems on the Cape were abundant then and probably far worse today. The Air Force training program at Otis National Guard in Bourne has contributed its share of collateral damage. The Boston Globe reported that the firing of ordnance released chemicals into the underground water and poisoned the water supply for the upper Cape. The planes often dumped their excess gasoline on the grounds of the base. A gallon of gasoline leaking from an abandoned gasoline tank can poison the water supply for a village. If the sands of the Cape absorb rainwater so easily, one wonders how much wastewater it absorbs as well. When a woman living four houses away from us turned on the water, foam filled her sink. Investigation showed it came from the laundromat near the pumping station, which pumped its wastewater deep into the ground.

Nevertheless, we came to love the Cape and our closeness to sky, sea and dune. The nearby pond had its share of snapping turtles and I did not have to fear polluting the pond with the remains of fish I had caught; snappers are scavengers and always take care of decaying flesh. We also had a pet turtle, a snapper who would show up for a free meal of fish scraps. But they are always hungry and will catch live things. Mallards nested on our pond. A flock would start in the spring with a dozen ducklings and end up with a couple by the end of summer. Mr. Turtle was the culprit. One day while sitting on the edge of the pond (the cottage was only 30 feet from the water) I heard the quacking of a mallard and watched it being pulled underwater. Mr. Turtle had a meal.

Long after I had left the area and was visiting on the lower Cape in Sandwich, I noticed many large sunfish in a small pond, many of the largest on their nests near shore. My friends loved fresh water sunfish and I offered to catch some. Anchoring a small rowboat in about 30 feet of water, I caught a dozen nice sunfish in a half hour, putting them on a stringer hanging below the bottom of the boat. When I pulled up the stringer to put another fish on, it seemed lighter. Then I noticed just the head of a fish, and I knew a turtle was at work. I thought (I was not thinking) I would entice it up to where I could grab its tail and drag it into the boat. It came to the surface still cutting off chunks of a fish. When I grabbed for its tail, there was a big swirl and its head was where its tail was in an instant. I made some quick fancy moves and avoided losing a finger or two to Mr. Turtle's lunch.

Cape stories abound, but I heard this unusual, true story and never forgot it. A parishioner set out on a cold, icy morning in his jeep to drive the 14 miles from Nauset inlet to Chatham inlet to hunt for ducks. He told his wife he would be back by noon. It was an easy drive down because the tide was falling with an hour to go before low tide. When noon came and went and he had not returned, his wife became alarmed and called the chief of police, Chet Landers, who called the fire chief, Larry Ellis. They set out in their jeep to look for the hunter.

They saw no sign of him and they felt under pressure to return quickly as it would soon be high tide. Five miles from the inlet, the high waves of the incoming tide forced them up on the snow-encrusted dunes and they were soon mired in ice and sand. While they were looking for a plank of driftwood to help pry themselves out, Larry said, "I smell smoke." His friend chided him, saying that after twenty-some years fighting fires, he would always smell smoke. But Larry said again, "I smell smoke."

Nearby there were several cabins on the outer beach, one just opposite the place where they had mired down. They decided to investigate and in the cabin they found the hunter nearly unconscious and half frozen. His jeep had been swamped by a giant rogue wave and it was never found. He had made his way five miles to the cabin where he was able to make a fire, but there was not enough wood to keep it going. The hunter lost several toes from frostbite but was always grateful to a fire chief who said, "I smell smoke."

Over the years, I had many fishing partners and one of the best was Jack. He and his wife, June, were lovers of the Cape. He had become a teacher and taught school in New York, but when the last bell of the year rang, he and June took off from the gate like two racehorses, heading for the Cape for the summer. Jack was an avid fisherman and fished hard to make enough money to call it a summer job, a job he loved. Even on stormy nights when any sane person would fish the surf and catch up on sleep, he was out on the water with his fishing gear.

I remember one puzzling summer. After many outings with Jack and two other friends, we did not catch a single fish. Jack said, "Someone is jinxing us. Maybe it's the preacher."

Earlier, we had enough confidence to propose catching a slew of stripers and freezing them so we could have a special bass dinner at the end of summer. But the jinx pattern kept up. Every time I went along, we got skunked.

"If we don't catch a bass today, it's because Wallen is a Jonah," said Jack.

Do you remember what his mates did in that story? They threw Jonah overboard and then they caught a fish. "Tonight," they declared, "was the night."

Well, it turned out I had a sick parishioner due for surgery the next morning and he had asked me to come and say prayers before he went to sleep. So I did. The next day Jack was packing up and came to the parsonage to say goodbye. He also predicted that I, alone, would never catch another bass until I got wet.

The following week another friend came to visit and I had promised him steamed clams. He went with me to Nauset Inlet and in low tide we spotted a bed of clams. He was in his swimming trunks but I was not. We stayed too long and the tide began to come up. I was going to take off my boots, but he said, "Get up on my shoulders and I will carry you back to shore." I did. Then he promptly stepped in a clam hole and I got soaking wet. The next night I caught a pair of 40-pound fish, which proved to them I was not a Jonah. But they never stopped calling me Jonah if we didn't catch any fish.

Jack never missed the 8 a.m. Sunday service at Orleans Methodist. I accused him one morning of sleeping through the sermon and he denied it, reciting the three-point outline we were taught in constructing a sermon at BU School of Theology.

Throughout my days on the Cape, I began playing an ever-larger role in alcohol counseling and becoming more skillful in handling such problems. Since I had seen so many addicted people, I was beginning to see patterns in what worked and what didn't in the process of overcoming these addictions.

Whiskey has its good points. My grandfather in West Virginia was poor but still paid $1.25 for his gallon of whiskey, not to guzzle down, but as a household item with multiple uses. It was valuable as a painkiller, which I discovered as a child when I was given whiskey to dull a toothache. In war, it was a useful anesthetic and in war and peace it was valuable in preserving food and could kill bacteria in water. But as we all know, alcohol has its dark side.

Growing up in the Methodist church, I was given a very strong message that alcohol is a killer, not a friend, and I could see that my parents never drank. I'm sure Mother was affected by her sister, aunt Wilmer, who disappeared on the streets of Washington as a young girl and died young. At the same time, my parents were sympathetic and helpful to those who had problems with alcohol. You may recall my mother brought my Uncle Junior to live with us for a year in order to help him recover from alcoholism. He told her it was the only thing that ever worked.

Many of my friends, at some point, had bouts with drinking when trouble knocked on the door. In college, it took a while but my friends accepted my stone cold sobriety. As my friendships expanded, I found myself in various informal support groups to help those with problems recover. Perhaps it was a natural thing to take my ministry in this direction. Or maybe it was a problem you just kept bumping into, especially as a minister.

Over the years, I have learned that recovery requires three things: An inner commitment to eliminate alcohol from your life, but you need friends to support you in this, and not your drinking friends. All the emotional and psychiatric resources that sustain us are found in our relationships so the second step is to build new relationships in a group. The AA community is one such group. So attend an AA meeting every day for 90 days. Out of that experience you may find someone with whom you feel comfortable and you will begin to support one another. The third requirement is for you to develop new activities that involve doing something for others. A critical issue here is for one to reestablish the integrity of his word, which addiction destroys.

Chapter 15

New Bedford

In 1961, I was assigned to be the pastor of Trinity Methodist Church in New Bedford. From a small Cape Cod church, I was plunged into an urban setting that couldn't have been more different from the leisurely, tranquil pace of Orleans. New Bedford, located in the southeastern corner of Massachusetts, is a coastal city with real character and a great history, but with more than its share of urban problems. It was the 1960s, after all, Vietnam was raging, students were protesting and all hell was about to break loose over our land. It affected our children, whatever their age.

New Bedford is an old whaling city whose economy still suffers from the loss of its major industries. When whaling died in the 1880's, textile mills sprung up and immigrants from Europe filled the mills. But in the 1920's the textile mills moved south for cheaper labor and the New England mills were in decline. The Great Depression finished them off. With textiles dead, the empty mills turned to the manufacture of garments after World War II. New immigrants arrived from Portugal and the Cape Verde Islands to work in the factories or on fishing boats, New Bedford's other great industry. The fishing industry often flourished, but has suffered its bad years too.

The Portuguese were the dominant group in the city and, at this time, had the highest rate of savings per capita in the country. But these savings came from a family structure that sometimes forced the children to drop out of school at 16 and go to work, turning their paychecks over to their parents. Not such a good idea when today those very factories are closed. Education is more valued today as a result.

Trinity Methodist was a landmark brick structure that dominated the skyline at the corner of Elm and County Streets. Its architecture is rare: four hanging suspended cones carried the weight of the roof. Its pipe organ is one of the finest in the nation. The sanctuary seated 800 people, but its membership was being bled to death by urban flight to the suburbs. The parsonage contained eleven rocking chairs, most of them gifts for a tax write-off.

Maple Street, home of the parsonage, was awash with children. John, our youngest son, was one of eight eight-year-old boys in the neighborhood. One of his friends was Jackie Marivel and they became "blood brothers." His father was head of the Welfare department and his sister Gloria would one day become active in the Civil Rights movement. She would go South and help to register black voters, a very brave thing to do. On the whole, John was adjusting and so was James, our middle child.

It was Charles, our oldest, who gave us problems. He was 12 when we moved from the Cape and he had loved it there. He would have hated any move to anywhere, and so he hated New Bedford almost immediately, but he found joy in the sixties culture. The Beatles were the rage and Charles fell for them in a big way, deciding he would play his guitar for the rest of his life—on Cape Cod in the summer, in Florida in the winter. He began playing regularly and made two friends who were also into music, Jerry S. and Alan L., boys who dominated the neighborhood group. Soon they gathered some friends and started a rock band, practicing on the third floor of the parsonage. From the beginning, they were good enough to cut a record, which might have become a financial success, but they did not follow through.

His interest in music didn't help Charles in other ways. He had less and less interest in school. In an effort to control his level of rebellion, I supported him and his friends and their music making. Jerry's father was a scalloper and owned a fishing boat, so he was at sea a lot. Alan's father had died and he was still angry about this loss. His mother had little control over him. He charged items at stores and she scolded him but she also paid the bills. His first year in New Bedford, Charles failed his courses and rebelled against all family rules. We were not alone with our problems.

My next-door neighbors had been honored as an ideal Catholic family, but they had family troubles too. Their oldest son decided to run away with his friend so he took money out of his college savings account and bought two plane tickets to Florida. If Charles had been there, he would have joined them. My neighbor was beside himself when he discovered his son was missing. I told him my schedule was free and I would pick the kids up when the police found them. Instead he learned they were in Florida so he had them flown back to New Bedford. They immediately became heroes to the rest of the kids.

It was the sixties, and schools were exploding across the nation.

Later that summer one of the boys stole his mother's car and took it for a joy ride. Charles was involved and lost his privilege to get his driver's license until he was 17. Alan, the drummer, was destructive any time he came into the house. He put 32 holes in the wall with a screwdriver on his way up to the third floor. He threw eggs from our refrigerator at John who was playing with his friends in the street.

When he spotted me after the screwdriver incident, he headed around the corner to his home at top speed. I was behind him and landed on the front porch exactly when he did. I was red-faced and very angry. I told his mother he no longer had my permission to be in my home if I wasn't there. And, furthermore, he could come inside only for band practice. I changed my schedule so I was home to prevent any after-school shenanigans and he kept his word. Not long after, he became involved in selling drugs in the neighborhood. Ten years later I counseled him through the Pastoral Care and Counseling program at the Inter-Church Council.

Things did not improve for Charles either. When he failed two years of school, our family was in crisis. We knew we had to get him out of the neighborhood and out of the city. I recall one day he skipped school and spent the day hiding out in a friend's garage. When he appeared that afternoon with a story, I read back to him what really went on that day and he was flabbergasted that I knew every detail. I believe this convinced him that we cared for him and would do whatever we had to in order to reach him.

After doing some research, we decided to send him to Tilton Prep School in New Hampshire. He knew he was at rock bottom and accepted our sending him away. As it turned out, this change in environment saved his life.

Meanwhile, the crisis was turning our lives upside down. I was earning $6,000 a year and the prep school cost $3,000 a year—half my salary. But we had to do it, so I resigned from the Methodist ministry to make more money. I looked to a new federal program that had recently opened its doors in New Bedford. The Job Corps was part of President Johnson's War on Poverty and I knew what they were about. I decided my experience would serve them well. I applied and got a job as a senior counselor at the

Rodman Job Corps in the south end of New Bedford. My salary would be $14,000, which more than doubled my church salary.

To be honest, my decision to leave the church had been brewing for some time. Perhaps it went back to my experience at West Roxbury when the bishop and the local church did not support my getting a Ph.D. while serving there. I was shocked by such small-mindedness and do not believe that sort of thing would happen today. The bishop did not accept my role as a counselor, the most important thing I did. Nor did I get over the shock of him asking me why I hadn't yet converted my wife. My ministry was not about converting people, certainly not my wife who has a mind of her own. I wanted to counsel people, help them in their daily struggles. And that is the direction I had been going for many years without ever quite saying—"This is my calling."

I was also troubled by the vote of a nationwide Methodist conference in which 400,000 black church members were put in a separate jurisdiction. My interest was in ending segregation in the church, but clearly this was not the end of racism. Sadly, I knew that someday I would leave the church. Everything came together at this moment—this was the time.

Meanwhile, our neighbor, Mr. Marivel, hired Chris as a social worker. She visited the homes of people who were eligible for welfare and she was so turned off by the dirt and smell, she resigned after a year to take a teaching job. She worked just blocks from the school and one day she walked home to get some materials. It was a day when the teachers had meetings and school ran for a half day. She found John at home with five other boys and girls and she smelled a strange odor. She asked what it was and John said his friend was burning incense.

"That doesn't smell like incense," she replied. "I know what you are doing,"

"They're smoking marijuana?" said John innocently. The purpose of the teachers' meeting that day involved drugs. A policeman burned some marijuana so the teachers could tell what it smelled like. Chris had a crash course.

With all our problems, we did have a few moments of serenity. Soon after moving to New Bedford, we bought a small cottage on the Cape. At first, we did not want to buy in Orleans because our presence might be a problem for the new minister—I was very sensitive about the issue of new ministers, old ministers—the two do not mix. However, our best buy was a cottage for sale on the edge of Boland Pond in the middle of Orleans. I could lay low as far as the church was concerned and spend my time fishing, which was the whole idea anyway. I borrowed $2,000 from my father and we bought it from the Snows, a couple that lived on the larger property. Our idea was to rent it out in the summer and that alone would pay the mortgage. Meanwhile, we would use it in the spring and fall. The kindly Mrs. Snow became our rental agent and Mr. Snow took care of the property. What a joy!

It worked perfectly. The pond was full of pickerel and yellow perch. Wildlife was abundant. Mallard ducks nested every spring and the ducklings became very tame. If you were sitting outside, they would arrive for dinner and peck your feet if you did not feed them. I bought a small rowboat and would catch 30 or 40 pickerel in the spring. Occasionally one would go in the cooking pot, but they were full of bones and no match for the other fish.

Orleans had many glacial pothole ponds like Boland. Two larger ones, Crystal and Baker, were stocked with trout and small mouth bass. In ancient times, the ocean broke through the sand dunes and formed tidal ponds, the salt water mixing with the freshwater ponds. Our cottage was such a joy in the years before the Cape developed as an over-the-top holiday and retirement Mecca.

For fifteen years, we had no problems. Then Mr. Snow died and Mrs. Snow sold her property. Soon nothing was safe. One spring, Christine went to the cottage with a friend to do some painting and returned saying there was something dead under the cottage. I investigated and found that an alcoholic had broken in during the winter, slept in the beds and urinated on the mattresses, then turned them over so you could not tell the origin of the odor. I found a rum bottle between the mattresses.

Life outdoors was not the same either with traffic now choking the highways. One weekend we went to the cottage to ready it for renters and discovered it was a four-hour journey from Brewster to the Cape Cod Bridge, only 25 miles away. Then there was the problem of ownership. I was spending most of my time taking care of the cottage instead of fishing. So we said a sad goodbye and put it on the market for $77,000. I suppose today it would be over three hundred thousand.

Meanwhile, back in New Bedford, it was time to change our address. We lived in a decidedly urban environment and our children needed more room to play. In 1966, we moved out of New Bedford into neighboring Dartmouth and bought a house on Hilltop Road for $19,000. It was a typical suburban neighborhood where many families planted arborvitae bushes to grow a fence and hence be shielded from their neighbors. The family next door decided they would not put up a fence and that created a big play area. But a week after we moved in, a ball landed in my other neighbor's yard and he sent his ten-year-old daughter to get that ball and bring it into his house. Our son John came in angry saying they took our ball. I had to talk to my neighbor.

At first, he wanted no ball playing at all because he was planting an Arborvitae fence and didn't want a broken branch marring its perfection. It took us several months to work out an agreement. I told him I would work with the kids and we would decide on some rules. If a ball landed in his yard and damaged a tree, I would be as upset as if it were a broken arm. As a result, over the years, the neighborhood children have shown respect for everyone's property as well as each other, and that has been a pleasure to behold.

An Arborvitae fence creates privacy but it also creates isolation. As it grows, it shuts out all face-too-face communication. Thank God for wild deer. They love it and will eat their way clear through such a fence.

As for fish stories, I had some great trips in my fishing boat with its 25-horse power motor, which I'd acquired in Orleans. I docked it at the marina on West Island in Fairhaven. Most memorable was a trip I took with my brother-in-law when we found ourselves in a school of feeding blue fish. He had never experienced that before.

One day I pulled into the parking lot at the same time as a car with Illinois plates. The driver stuck his head out and asked for suggestions on how to go about catching a striped bass. He had brought his ten-year-old son all this way and so far, no luck. I said that the two old retired fishermen sitting on the porch of the marina might help.

"We won't tell you but we'll tell your son," they replied, and asked the driver to return to his car. Then they said in a loud enough voice for everyone to hear, "Send your father to get some limburger cheese, a stick, and a brace and bit. You drill a hole in the water, place the limburger cheese on the side of the hole and stand there with the stick. When that old striper sticks his head out, hit it with the stick." The father heard the directions, grabbed his son and roared out of the driveway.

Rodman Job Corps

The Rodman Job Corps was a federal program for teenagers 16 and over who had dropped out of school and were looking at continued poverty and a jobless future. It was a residential, remedial program to help them develop academic and job skills so they could become employed. The

Center, located in New Bedford's South End, was actually run by IBM. Of the 750 teens who arrived in New Bedford, over half were blacks from the South and over half could not effectively read. They had problems with alcohol, drugs and anger. The majority did not have fathers to guide them and act as role models. They had serious medical and dental needs. The program offered them hope and a way out.

There were many Job Corps spread throughout the nation and New Bedford was not the only city that resisted the small invasion of young men from the outside. New Bedford had one advantage over the other Job Corps. It offered training in computer programming and offset printing, and students who took these subjects were more reliable and motivated. Rodman took in many transfers from Job Corps in other areas because of the uniqueness of this program. The program was based on a student-counselor relationship and I was hired as one of sixteen counselors, eventually becoming Director of Counseling Services. Counselor tutors were in charge of the academics.

Many flaws plagued the buildings that housed the Rodman students. None was worse than the design of the dining hall, which had one chow line for 650 hungry students. The black students insisted on wearing their hats everyday, and everywhere, including the chow line. The rule was—no hats in the dining room. The only ones who could enforce the rule were the counselors because we had relationships with the students and we used the power of eye contact and quiet persuasion. When I was on dining hall duty, I would stand in one position and if a student entered with a hat on, I would not take my eye off his hat until he removed it. It worked most of the time, but put an administrator on the line and it did not work.

The job wasn't easy. We had to learn to communicate with the inner city black students who had developed a sub-culture language based on white profanity. The key word was mother-fucker. If the boys used it in public, it touched off clashes with local police and citizens. In their own culture, the word had seven different meanings, from the worst insult to the highest compliment.

Rodman tried to get students involved in the community, but it was difficult. To begin with, there was a population explosion among teenagers in the general population and given these revolutionary times, people were wary. Downtown New Bedford was a popular place for local kids to congregate on Thursday nights and the city seemed accommodating at first. Churches tried to step in too. Hard to believe but the streets were sometimes packed with 3,000 teenagers. On one occasion, the

Congregational Church sponsored a rock band and admitted 200 kids. Another 150 could not get in and started trouble in the streets. The band had to be canceled.

Later that year, Trinity Methodist Church initiated a program with the help of Rodman staff and students. The beauty of Trinity was its location a block away from the most crowded area in town so we could actually run a successful program. We had an inter-racial band with local kids cooperating with Rodman kids. James Bean, my son, and James Richards, a black student at Rodman, were co-chairmen. A New Bedford policeman was on duty along with Rodman staff. When there was conflict, the students handled it.

We did the best we could but the Job Corps students, poor and black, could not easily integrate into the community. They found it difficult to have any sort of social life because people were frightened of them. Therefore, Rodman made arrangements for busloads of students to go to Poland Springs, Maine, on weekends where there was a girls' Job Corps with 1800 recruits, and they could finally have a social life.

Washington was always trying to micromanage from a distance and we received two messages we were supposed to enforce: Discharge any student who is caught with a weapon and anyone the staff thinks might be gay. These mandates created a field day for the dorm counselors. They were a perfect way to get rid of student troublemakers in the dorm and a list of names quickly appeared.

I sent a memo to the dorm counselor and to Washington.

"Please define a weapon," I wrote. "And tell us how we are to get rid of a weapon that every student has—a fist." As for being gay, I asked for a list of the characteristics of a gay person and included a list of my own but used the counselors as bait.

"My boss has a funny approach to the bowling alley."

"A counselor walks funny."

"Another staff member has a high tenor voice."

After I sent these requests to Washington, we heard nothing further.

The presence of so many young men in town caused social upheaval in New Bedford. The city is 13 miles long and 3 miles wide and the South End alone had to absorb the students. The police were swamped by the numbers. Rodman tried to help out by creating student patrols, trained to intervene in trouble. Their role was critical in one particular incident involving a white student. He had "borrowed" a few long black coats popular with the black students and had been selling them. He would then borrow another to cover the demand to return a coat.

He fled the Center when he got in too deep. We had to notify the local police that he was probably armed. The student patrol had some idea where he was headed and got their first opportunity to apprehend the runaway before the police found him. The Center believed that police would shoot first and ask questions later.

Another young man, William, was accused of pulling a gun on two other students in the chow line. The only witnesses were the accusers and many had their doubts it had happened at all. Since Rodman was located on federal lands, the FBI took care of such internal problems. I remember handing William his graduation diploma while two FBI men were putting him in handcuffs. William would be in jail until his 21st birthday. An awful waste.

The most talented tutor-counselor on the staff was David DiCicco. A psychology major in college, David took to the work like a fish to water and I was privileged to supervise him. He volunteered time to run groups, one of them a creative writing group that was popular. He was a master at performing the dual role of tutor-counselor, the concept that guided the center, as he helped prepare students to function in that most middle-class of institutions, "the office." After a year at Rodman, David felt so strongly that this was his field that he resigned to get his master's degree, then returned after completing his work. Eventually he got his doctorate in child psychology in San Diego.

He and his girlfriend Vicky were married in Boston in a Catholic church and after the ceremony we all stayed at a local motel for two days of celebration before they went on their honeymoon.

David is now well known in his field, and I believe his influence is alive in those students today.

An ongoing theme in this memoir is "the power of small groups," which was tested once again at Rodman. We formed a problem-solving group made up of some of the most talented students who had demonstrated leadership abilities. They called themselves "the social engineers" and were given a fixed budget to buy furniture for a student lounge. Through negotiations and comparing prices, they nearly doubled the amount of furniture for the project and received the accolades of their fellow Corpsmen.

One Monday morning our staff read in the newspaper, along with everyone else, that Rodman was closing. The funding was pulled by the Johnson Administration to secretly pay for the Vietnam War. Some good things were accomplished in spite of the problems. IBM hired every single trainee who had taken computer programming and offset printing. Others I'm sure went back to their ghettos and languished. All the valuable information we had gathered on the condition of the poor has disappeared in Washington vaults, unavailable for research and study.

Rodman Job Corps was a social experiment on a grand scale, in keeping with President Johnson's Great Society vision. School dropouts were a drain on the resources of the nation. Fix the problem through education and job training and the boys and girls would become assets rather than liabilities. The costs would be recovered in the future when the kids would lead better lives and enjoy higher incomes. The program was ambitious, taking these boys out of their environment and introducing them to a new world, such as it was.

As the director and senior counselor, I had to find employment for the disheartened staff, which I did. I was offered a job by IBM to be a counselor to employees at a plant in Raleigh, North Carolina but decided not to accept because my family was now doing well in Dartmouth. Dr. Fred Hinman advised me to accept a job at the new mental health center in Fall River.

On March 1, 1968, the Rodman Job Corps closed. I was the last person to leave.

In New Bedford, I became involved in settling conflicts between the city's Portuguese residents and the Cape Verdeans, descendants and immigrants from the Cape Verde Islands. Due to the fishing and textile industries, New Bedford had a majority Portuguese population. A smaller group of Cape Verdeans, of Portuguese and African descent, also made New Bedford their home, and the conflict between the two groups was ongoing. The Cape Verdeans were listed in the census as white, which was an insult to those who considered themselves black. It was considered a social disgrace for the daughter of a Portuguese family to marry a Cape Verdean. One prominent Portuguese family had a daughter who fell in love with a Cape Verdean. Her father said if she continued to see him, he would disown her. I counseled this family over a long period and she went on to marry the Cape Verdean. In six months her mother died of a heart attack and, of course, the family attributed the tragedy to the marriage. Years later, if I blundered and asked the man how his daughter was doing, he would reply, "What daughter?"

I performed many mixed marriages, religious and cultural. At a meeting during the height of the Civil Rights revolution, I was asked whether I was more related to Martin Luther King or Bull Connor. I would certainly hope it was Martin Luther King. I was learning to be bullish in standing up for progressive values.

Corrigan Mental Health Center

After spending two years with the Rodman Job Corps, I was again looking for work. Fortunately, I had a varied background encompassing many skills that were much needed in the world of the sixties. Academically, I had a master's degree in the sociology of religion and had ministered to five congregations while becoming increasingly involved in counseling. I had done marriage counseling, alcohol and drug counseling; I had counseled troubled youths in the Job Corps. I had experience as a minister, counselor and social worker so I was well suited for what might come next. Or was I?

The year was 1968 and the growing problem in society was drugs. I began my new job at the Corrigan Mental Health Center in Fall River as a counseling specialist. But drugs are tricky and these were dangerous waters. My job at Corrigan was dealing with the growing drug problems among teenagers.

I was promptly invited to Mrs. Roberts' seventh grade class to do a presentation and sound out the kids on drugs. They spoke freely. They had some interest in drugs and were aware that some kids were using street drugs. Fortunately, I was invited back for the next three years and could gauge the depth of the problem and how it changed from year to year. The second year the kids were much more curious about drugs. Some had smoked pot but they had a sense of caution. The third year I found the kids were outright enthusiastic about drugs and would not pass up the opportunity to try something. The fourth year they had gone back to a more cautious position. This change of mind and heart came from an unexpected source. Many had known older youths who had experimented and endured unexpected, sometimes harrowing experiences. A lesson from the horse's mouth.

At Corrigan Mental Health Center, I plunged headfirst into the drug problem. We were dealing with kids who had gone to pot parties in large groups. Some would bring handfuls of pills from the family medicine cabinet, mix them in a bowl, take a few and see what happened. If the group could reassure those who were having a bad reaction, they would be okay. If not, there was panic. When they overdosed, they were sent to Corrigan. Being a counselor at Corrigan wasn't easy. We had a battle on our hands and little to go on in treating these kids.

Crisis after crisis hit the center before all the staff had even been hired, but we managed to get a team together and went into small group counseling sessions, which became a major tool. Again, I saw the solidarity and power of small group counseling. At Corrigan, it was groups, groups, groups. We volunteered to do group counseling in the evenings so I led one in marriage counseling and another for parents of teenagers in trouble. I teamed up with a nurse to work with teenagers sentenced to group counseling by the courts. Each had been in court on a stubbornness complaint initiated by their parents—five girls and one boy in the initial group. They came for counseling once a week and in the initial sessions they left the building vandalized. Things got better when we began winning their confidence and they realized they were being heard and helped.

One of the girls asked to bring a friend. We said yes and she brought her entire gang. They dominated the group sessions for weeks but they also became the source of valuable information. When the chief of police in a Fall River suburb said there was no drug use in his town, the group named a dozen kids they knew who were heavy drug users. They identified police officers that were abusing their authority in dealing with young people, which led to changes in personnel in certain trouble spots. I counseled many sons and daughters of New Bedford police officers. The state, becoming ever more savvy, began to sponsor self-help groups for kids.

Revolutionary forces were pulling youngsters in every direction away from their middle-class origins. They raged against the war in Vietnam. They raged against the sterility and comforts of the middle-class, which they themselves enjoyed. They raged against their parents and their parents' values. They raged against their schools and colleges. A sexual revolution was in full swing. Drugs were rampant. Thousands were on the run. Many had pick-up trucks, which seemed to fit their lifestyles. It was a crazy time.

As a member of the staff of Corrigan for four years, I came upon confused, disbelieving parents who felt lost and helpless. Often they did not want to know what their children were up to. They were reluctant to call Jane's parents to see if their daughter was really at a sleepover. They avoided cleaning up their kids' rooms, fearful of what they might find. They didn't want to check pockets or eavesdrop on phone calls. The parents were desperate for help but absolutely at a loss as to what to do.

Groups of as many as 30 kids were living together with no parents at all in some big houses in New Bedford and Fall River. It was, after all, the time of the commune and they didn't have to go to Vermont to live communally. They could have it all right here and now.

A lot more was going on at Corrigan than kids and drugs. Originally a mental health clinic, it was renamed to honor Dr. Corrigan for his long service to the city, and was headed by a psychiatrist, Dr. Lockwood Town. Its budget eventually called for 125 staff members; at the moment it had four: a social worker, a nurse, a receptionist and a clerk. I was the first addition to the staff, and we were at the forefront of a major change in social welfare in Massachusetts. The movement of mental health patients out of the gigantic state-run institutions had begun. Those who were able would now live in group homes in the community. This was new for everyone and our services were greatly needed.

For example, at one time Taunton Hospital had 2200 patients. Until now, the message of the mental health system was, "Send us your retarded and your mentally ill and we will take care of them—they will be out of sight for the rest of their lives." Up to 1954, a person in a state mental institution had no civil or legal rights. Referral to a mental hospital was likely to be a life sentence; less than ten percent of those admitted were ever discharged. The hospitals were holding centers—for life. Dr. Richard York, a psychiatrist employed by the Department of Mental Health, chaired a group that created a Bill of Rights for mental patients.

The movement didn't come about overnight. Two Harvard psychiatrists estimated that only ten percent of the programs at Taunton could qualify as treatment. Taunton was delivering custodial care at great cost. The cries for reform mounted and were heard in a society already in the midst of great social change.

We developed many new programs to address the resulting problems. Among them, we trained local police officers to learn how to talk a mentally ill person out of jumping off the Braga Bridge. They role-played and were judged by their peers on whether they had succeeded.

As the discharge of Taunton patients assigned to Fall River increased, it became apparent that certain staff members maintained a private practice on the side and this was an easy way to increase their clientele. They had a wealth of clients at their fingertips and were making deals with inmates. If an inmate agreed to see them in their private practice, they would be quickly discharged. I found one woman, a social worker on the staff at Taunton, to be very depressed and suffering from social isolation. I suggested she attend our day care program at Corrigan. She agreed, then said she had to have her therapist's approval. Her therapist was angry and she quickly canceled. She had been seeing him for years and, I guess, he was not about to give her up. Business is business.

Many old Massachusetts cities had lost their industrial base and people needed to be retrained. The state stepped in and created several community colleges, among them Bristol Community College in Fall River. Within three years of its opening, BCC had 3,000 students. I jumped in too and taught an evening course in social problems to students age 18 to 50. The textbook was ten years old and did not cover several revolutions which were taking place right before our eyes. I organized the class into teams and had the students do their own research, which they reported on in class. Among them were the Emancipation of Women from their traditional roles, the Black Revolution, the Sexual Revolution and, yes, Television. Hard to believe that television is that young. Computers and the Information Revolution lay in wait down the road.

Television broadcasting was being brought to New Bedford through a tower and station at the corner of County and Spring Streets. I assembled my class on a freezing cold December night in the station so they could share this moment. Not that I thought TV was a good thing, but it was historic for the New Bedford area. A young engineer scrambled up the tower to hook up the system, and, amazingly, the station began broadcasting. I discovered that this young man was from the Cape and had worked as a plumber. Lo and behold, he and his partner had drilled the well at the Orleans parsonage and neglected to tell me we could run a hose from my neighbor's outside faucet to our house. Even now, I was not quite ready to laugh.

That week was historical for another reason. The owner of the newspaper and TV station had hired a black engineer as manager of the new station. This may seem commonplace today but in those days it was a nice shock to the system. The new manager did not want to live in the ghetto but was turned away from renting or buying a house in white neighborhoods. Finally, the owner of the station journeyed into a white neighborhood, bought a house and the black family moved in. Meanwhile, the black man's difficulty inspired a group of us to create a new organization called the Workshop for Equality.

Members of the Jewish community played a major part and our goal was to integrate the neighborhoods. Most meetings were held in the home of Daniel and Helga Finger, two people who felt strongly enough about the issue to do something. The committee urged citizens to join the workshop.

Several hundred people signed a petition that appeared in the newspaper saying they were willing to work at integrating their neighborhoods.

Progress was being made, but sometimes it came hard. A couple from Trinity Methodist Church, both of them blind, were hired by the state of California (more progress) and they put their Fairhaven house on the market. A black sergeant who was heading for Vietnam put a binder on the house and all hell broke loose in the neighborhood. The blind woman called to inform me that her neighbors were accusing her of being a traitor. The realtor had also received a nasty call. The sergeant called the State Office Against Discrimination and was told, "If you need legal action, the best lawyer in New Bedford belongs to a group called Workshop for Equality." We were intent on resolving this without the courts. A member of the Workshop lived in the development and called a meeting of the neighbors. When the black family moved in, there were neighbors ready to welcome them.

Chapter 16

Civil Rights Legislation of the Sixties

With so much of society in upheaval, what better time to pass Civil Rights legislation that would finally give blacks their equal rights as citizens and human beings. The death of President Lincoln perhaps postponed the reconstruction of the South for 150 years but now the passage of the Civil Rights legislation in the 1960s gave black people some control over their destiny. The Reverend Martin Luther King led the crusade and President Lyndon Johnson got the legislation passed. Equal rights in education. Equal rights in housing. Equal voting rights and equal civil rights. The laws were passed but there would still be many battles ahead.

As one who grew up in West Virginia, I lived with the caste system and knew it wasn't right, but as a kid there was little I could do. It seemed to me there were three forces that sustained the caste system. The first was economic, which I myself experienced. As a teenager, I was hired one summer by local farmers to gather hay with a pitchfork and I earned $1.50 a day. Any black who worked alongside me was paid only a dollar a day. The second benefit to the white community was sexual. A black girl could not say no to a white man, and a black man could not defend his woman. I also had experience with this, albeit second hand.

Back in the summer of 1945, I was a member of a Methodist caravan. Five of us—a counselor and four white college students, two male and two female, were missionaries to seven communities in South Carolina. Our goal was to help a group of young people build a facility that would be of use to children of all colors in the community. We were welcomed into six of the seven communities but shunned by the seventh because of a recent terrible incident. A week before we arrived, a young black man arrived home to find a white man raping his wife. He shot and killed the white man. We tried to find out the fate of the black man but we could not. I believe he was murdered and the community covered it up. You could have cut the tension in that community with a knife. The caste system was still in full swing in many Southern states.

In seminary in Boston, I once heard a lecture by an educator from a Quaker school in Putney, Vermont who told a story of three schools that shaped our history, for better or worse. I never forgot them.

The Highland Folk School in the mountains of Tennessee educated Rosa Parks, the woman who refused to obey the segregation law requiring blacks to move to the back of the bus.

The University of Georgia had as president, one Moses Waddel, who was a southern segregationist and stern taskmaster. Besides disdaining blacks, he disdained women too. He often said, "A woman's brain is too soft to educate." This man's influence was strong among those who persuaded the South to secede from the union, which led the Confederacy into the Civil War.

William and Mary College in Virginia is the third, but ranks number one. When the school tried to hire a man, a Quaker named George Whythe as a law professor, at first he refused because he had no formal education—he had been taught by his mother. But he finally accepted the challenge.

When he stood before the class of southern plantation boys, he said:

"Good morning gentlemen. So you want to be lawyers? There are changes a-coming. There may be a new nation. Go back to your rooms and think about what I've said. The class is dismissed."

The next day he simply said, "I have checked your records and found that each of you are the firstborns of your families. Where are your brothers and sisters? Shall they be educated too?"

The third morning, he said, "Each of you is from a slaveholding family. If you could write the laws, how would you right the laws about slavery?"

Then one morning he said, "You privileged few. In the new nation every citizen must be a statesman."

And so we were blessed with this school's legacy. In these classes were Thomas Jefferson, James Madison and one other founding father.

I never forgot that speech, just the remaining founding father.

Chapter 17

The Cape and Islands

I have often referred to beautiful Cape Cod as a "sick sandbar," particularly during my time as pastor in Orleans when I became aware of how dire the situation was. At the time, the Cape had no mental health services at all. People suffered—isolation was a common theme—and the towns were isolated fiefdoms. A surprising number of people had never crossed the canal to connect with bigger eastern cities. The wife of one state official was born in Pocasset and had never been to Provincetown.

As a pastor in Orleans, I tried hard to get people and organizations connected and to foster cooperation between them but I could not. First I attempted to form a council of churches and failed. I could not get anyone to travel more than ten miles from their own town. In Orleans there were three doctors. I could not get them to support one another including covering another's town when one went on vacation. And Cape Cod Hospital was just as parochial. Fewer than half of the doctors had practicing privileges. In other words they could not treat their own patients when they were in the hospital.

Many Cape doctors were refugees from problems they had developed in other communities and brought along with them. My family doctor in Orleans went on a bender once a year for two or three weeks, but he would be fine and available for the rest of the year. During one of these lapses, my son slit his eyelid in an accident. When I took him to Dr. Gillespie, he was drunk enough that I was tempted to head for the hospital 20 miles away. The doctor assured me he could put a clamp on the cut. I consented and he successfully did it. On the way home I said to my seven-year-old, "The doctor caused more pain than was necessary because he had been drinking." The doctor had been his hero. "That's all right," he said. Everyone has something that hurts." At that point, the tyke was going to be a minister, a missionary, a doctor or dentist.

Finally, the state took notice of the sad situation on Cape Cod and decided to create a full program of services. Dr. Hinman, a state psychiatrist, asked me to consider the job of setting it up. My resume fit the job perfectly, well, almost perfectly. I needed a master's degree and so I wrote to Boston University and asked what I had to do to convert the credits I'd acquired toward a doctorate to a master's. After examining my records, they said I only had to send in $35 and be there for graduation. "Why in hell didn't you do it ten years ago?" they asked. And that's how I became the Associate Director of Social Services for the Cape and Islands.

The job was part-time and I was employed for four years. Though I was paid $14,000 a year, I did not give up my work at Corrigan. With all my complaining about the lack of services on the Cape, it was now my responsibility to do something about it! In fact, the area's director position had not been funded and so, unofficially, I was the director. The Cape was booming with new population but remained impoverished in so many ways. There was no public transportation. A new retirement community had just opened in Falmouth and residents had a hard time getting anywhere. As for me, I had to drive everywhere, which meant putting 100,000 miles on a new Dodge Dart. I operated the first two years out of my car. I had no office, phone, or secretarial services.

The new state commissioner had surveyed the structure of the Department of Mental Health and declared it was unmanageable without changes; for example, programs were to be initiated nearest the site of performance. Another required the area office not be bypassed in the decision-making process, and, since the Department provided an office in the National Park in Eastham, that meant I was to spend many a night there to save a trip home to New Bedford. Occasionally it was necessary for us to meet at night.

There were, in fact, several private clinics funded by private foundations. They had dedicated workers who had operated on shoestring budgets but were a part of what I learned to call fiefdoms. They had mixed feelings about a deluge of money from the state, which would take control away from them. One of these clinic directors, whose salary was nearly doubled by state funding through my office, began to oppose my management of the developing resources. I knew I would need assistance from the community if we were to move forward. My first official act was to form a professional review team whose job it was to interpret to the community our plans and goals. It was a defensive move and paid off nicely. The public was mostly on our side.

Because of a lack of public transportation, people were often shut-ins, especially in winter. So the mantra was, "Come over to my place and have a drink." It figured that the first burst of money from the state would be to treat alcoholism, especially for mothers at home with children. This meant fishermen's families. The women and children coped for weeks at a time with their men out to sea.

While the Cape languished and problems festered, the nearby island of Martha's Vineyard enjoyed the best of mental health services under the leadership of Dr. Mazer. Seldom did a resident of the Island have to go off-Island for treatment of any kind. A Cape committee had been formed to help me, and I was happy that it was led by members from Martha's Vineyard.

An active committee on alcoholism emerged with representatives from most of the towns and the Islands. Four groups were vying for the funds in a fierce competition. Members of one group were unhappy enough to write poison pen letters and start a rumor I was having an affair with the director we eventually hired.

The first detox unit was set up in Pocasset. The committee took the position that a "controlled" director of the unit be hired, that is, a controlled alcoholic who was not addicted. I hired Paul to develop the additional capacity of the detox unit and founded a halfway house for recovering alcoholics in Falmouth. Years after I left the Cape, he was still in charge.

I had a feisty relationship with the Boston office. They had supplied me with ten different studies of the needs of the Cape and not one offered treatment options or the means of addressing the problems. By the end of the first year, I had developed enough clout to ignore their unending requests. If they had any more requests (and no ways and means), I said I would meet them at the canal and drop them in. If they were coming to provide the money for services, I would meet them at the canal with a band.

At the end of the first year, I had a little more breathing room, but not much. Amazingly, a council of churches was organized and its director, David Grogan, was a social activist. He offered me cheap space for an office and we became a team. One day a man walked in and handed me a check for $10,000. He said, "Here is my time and money. I believe my two schizophrenic sons cannot get well at home. We need a half-way house for kids with such problems." We agreed and gladly accepted the money.

Luck was on our side again. Two structures had to be moved to make way for the enlargement of the steamship authority, and they were given to us for our halfway house.

We all worked together for opening day, and one of our benefactor's sons was among the first group admitted. David was chairman of the committee that managed the house but I happened to be in the office when a woman arrived saying she wanted to do something. I mentioned several items and referred her to David. She handed him a check for $32,000, and life was no longer simple for him and the halfway house. The lady felt she was buying more than the house, she was buying influence and favoritism toward her sons.

By my third year in this job, we were being swamped by the thousands of young people on the road. This was the sixties, after all, and Provincetown was a Mecca for them. In six months, we treated 600 young people and over a hundred had a venereal disease. To find out whether the grapevine was informing these young people of our services, I would pick up hitchhikers and try to find out.

One young man was obviously high and before I could inquire he said to me, "You got to get ready."

"Get ready for what?" I asked.

"Get ready for the coming of Jesus."

"I am ready," I said, which was a mistake.

"You got to get ready," he shouted.

"I am ready," I told him. "There is not one thing in my life I would change this day."

"Let me out," he yelled. I stopped the car and he got out shaking his fist and shouting, "You got to get ready."

My fourth year was focused on finishing the blueprints for the mental health center that would serve the Cape and Islands. There were heated debates about many issues, for instance, the plans called for including Wareham, which is not on the Cape at all. We also argued over where the new center should be located. I supported Pocasset since it was the geographic center of the area. Others thought differently.

Most of my time though, I spent getting required changes in the buildings. The corridors were too small to accommodate wheel chairs and had to be redesigned, thus reducing the space. This, of course, was a big item, but as you might imagine, the hundreds of details we had to attend to just made your head spin.

Chapter 18

Revival House

While I labored on the Cape, the Corrigan staff continued to expand services in the community. These social experiments were exploding across the state and turning somersaults to meet the needs of troubled kids. One of their bravest and riskiest moves was to open "Revival House," a residential facility for delinquent boys who were rejected by their families and communities.

In the first three years, both the building and program were in shambles due to an inept director. The students were out of control. My son James and his wife were hired as house parents, and the year they served probably helped destroy their marriage. A survey taken at the time revealed that not a single marriage survived the pressures of such an experiment.

I was asked to return to Fall River and manage the facility, and I certainly should have known better than to walk into the abyss. The program's first mistake was to allow those in charge to buy a house in the Highlands in Fall River, the city's most exclusive area. Not the best place for a home for delinquent boys. Two agencies had jurisdiction over the program and therein lay a host of problems. One department accepted the hot water level in the shower room, but the Department of Education required that it be 10 or 15 degrees hotter. It was madness. Because it was a state-funded program and rigid about such things, I had to modify the building or programs every year in order to meet the new state requirements. Often I threw my own money into it with the state's promise to eventually pay.

The neighborhood was friendly enough, but the residents made it clear they had the resources to evict us if we were trouble. I was in court once a month defending the school from nuisance charges due to noise, which required the services of a lawyer. Youth Services was willing to put the legal costs in the budget—next year.

The first crisis appeared immediately. The assistant director had added two names of students who had received no services during the month and I ordered that their names be removed. My budget was based on the number of days the students were in class and he basically wanted us to cook the books. The names were removed but later he added them again, which was illegal and would have put me in jeopardy. I fired him. He later opened his own school and appeared to be very successful.

The major challenge was to hire staff that could handle the kids. One applicant was Arnie J. who was working at a pricey school but quit when he was denied a raise. During the interview, he requested that he work on the job for two weeks to show what he could do. He was a controller and, in those two weeks, he actually had the residence in control.

Running the school was more difficult than just handling the residence, however. Arnie ruled by power; he could not work with a team. My experience taught me that control came out of relationship.

It was the cook that gave me the most problems of all. I had hired him for a CETA position (the Comprehensive Employment and Training Act) and he turned out to have a drug problem. I learned I could not fire him and he was enraged at my attempt to do so. His scruffy bunch of friends began to show up at Revival House.

In the midst of these events, someone threatened to hurt Arnie's mother as she drove to the factory where she worked. Without my knowledge, Arnie visited a member of a motorcycle gang in Fall River to warn them what would happen if threats against his mother were carried out.

At the same time, one of our students came to my office to tell me that friends of the cook were loading food from our freezer into their station wagon. I called the police. One of the two was so high on drugs, he hardly knew what he was doing. Arnie then told me what he had done. What a mess—I expected trouble and got it. Two weeks later, when I opened the door to Revival House, the interior was torn apart, the basement flooded from broken toilets, sewage everywhere, office equipment destroyed. I confronted Arnie and asked him what he was going to do.

"Nothing. If I do anything more, they will set the building on fire with the kids in it."

It was time to replace Arnie and look for a team builder.

Though it took five years, we really did build a team that could handle the boys. One of the most impressive was Charlie Toulan. He had recently left the shelter of a Catholic retreat and applied for the job. At this point, I was ready to throw in the towel unless a miracle occurred. And guess what? A miracle occurred with the arrival of Charlie.

"What are you doing getting these kids up at 7 a.m.?" he asked when he reviewed the schedule. "Teenagers love to sleep in. It's part of their rebellion, and they will get up at their leisure."

Well, Charlie seemed to have a way with the boys so I basically put him in charge while I went home to get away from it all and rethink everything. When I returned, I couldn't believe what I saw. Since there were two buildings and sixteen kids, Charlie had them divided into small working groups. The kids were actually studying and working. Amazing.

"You like to fish?" Charlie would say to me. "Take a kid fishing as often as possible. No one ever taught them these skills. They have no culture of doing things. Teach them."

"Yes, yes." I ended up taking a group of kids to my hometown of Moorefield, a rural scene new to most of them. They didn't know what to make of it. But we plunged in, introduced them to another world, and that was the important thing. They needed to see other ways than their narrow one of city streets where they did nothing but hate each other and fight over turf.

This was a dangerous time for the school. In spite of all the problems, I had the support of an unusual board of directors. During the last two years, trying to keep bankruptcy at bay, the chair of the board, Bob Bradley and I would go to the bank and we'd sign loan agreements with our signatures in order to meet the payroll. Bob was an insurance agent and he loved fishing. When he was on the board, he met Joan and they fell in love. I performed their wedding. His first wife was present and happy and so were his two sons and friends. Our friendship deepened.

One day Craig Lindell, who owned Fairhaven Corporation, was complaining about his insurance agent and I suggested that he talk to Bob. The next week Bob came to my office

"You want a boat? You want a trip to Europe? That recommendation of yours led to the largest policy in the history of this company." From then on, he had a nickname for me—the Godfather.

But the demise of Revival House was soon to come anyway. The Department of Youth Services decided to fund only one school in each area. Fall River had three schools for delinquent youths at the time, two with long histories and big endowments; I was new and operating on a shoestring. We decided to transfer Revival House to New Bedford and work with the Department of Social Services, where the director agreed to fund six positions.

Then, overnight, my life was upside down. The funding for the positions had been pulled to give step raises to existing staff, and I was not informed. I learned the news from a true friend in the Boston office. On September 1, 1981, I declared bankruptcy and closed the program. I had continually thrown in my own money, trying to keep the program going. My gamble that the state would keep its word cost me $45,000, which was the amount I had personally invested in Revival House. At that point, I expected to sell the buildings and recoup my losses, but we were at the beginning of a mild recession. For two years I had to maintain the two properties at my own expense, then sell them at half their market value.

Two students at Revival House I will always remember. One was a young black man from the South End of Boston who had grown up on the streets. The quietness at night was threatening to him. He needed the rumble of the streetcar and the noise of traffic. When I took a group to our farm in West Virginia and we visited a nearby dairy farm, he saw cows hooked up to milking machines and was uncomfortable with how a cow gave milk. When one opened up with a splatter of manure, he swore he would never drink milk again. One look at a chicken processing factory and he said he was done with eating chickens.

The second student was George. He had been committed to the Youth Service program because he was charged with arson in three serious fires. He was also subject to seizures. He was nearing his seventeenth birthday and becoming more depressed. His seizures were increasing, especially after being told he could never get a driver's license. He was evaluated in Boston and diagnosed with epilepsy. After completing a battery of tests, a doctor said to him, "George, go get your driver's license." It changed his life.

I needed some revival to help change my life. When all else failed, there was fishing. Another friend from graduate school, Bob Treese, loved to fish and, over the years, we bonded over the casting rod, perhaps more than we ever did as theologians. We savored our fishing time. Chris and I met Bob and Marie Treese at BU. He had given up a successful career as an engineer in Chicago to become a preacher. "Our country needs social engineers more than industrial engineers," he said. His wife Marie was not so sure.

"What would you think if I quit my job, sold our house and I went to seminary and become a preacher?" he asked out of the blue one day.

"I don't like the idea," she replied calmly but firmly, "and I hope you never mention the subject again."

Later when she had a chance to mull it over, she did an about turn. "I think you'd better quit your job, sell the house and get going. We may not be happy until we do."

It was brave of her as they had two daughters and a life hard to leave, but she did it and it all worked. That's how I came to know Bob, one of my most determined fishing companions. One day he called with a plan.

"How would you like to meet me at the Cape Cod Canal for an overnight? I want to teach my friend how to cast for big bass in the canal. We'll stay overnight at the campground and Marie will pack bacon and eggs for breakfast."

Things were going well until we realized the bacon and eggs were missing and we'd have to go without breakfast. Standing on the banks of the canal, we began casting the heavy plugs to attract larger fish. Bob's friend was catching on and we spread out so we would have more room to cast. My lure was sitting on the mowed grass and just as I was getting ready a skunk appeared. I called to Bob to see if we could scare it away and it left but came right back when I began to cast again. I picked up a small stone and hit the skunk gently on the head, or so I thought. It rolled over on its back, feet kicking in the air. When it came to, it let loose with its spray. The wind carried the scent down to Bob who let out a yell, dropped his rod and took off. The smell lasted several hours. I thought I'd lost a friend, but he laughed about me being a straight shooter.

We didn't catch a bass that day but we caught something better. We used a piece of squid for bait and within an hour found a lobster nibbling away on it. We set our net behind it and caught it. Altogether, we caught six lobsters, boiled them over a fire and had them for breakfast. Only later did we learn it was illegal to take them without a license. Anyway, they beat bacon and eggs.

It wasn't the best of times. It was 1972 and I was 50 years old, without a job, and had worked in the field of social services for many years without the necessary credentials. My master's degree was in the sociology of religion, which qualified me for very little. I suspected I wouldn't get many responses to my resume so I decided to create a role for myself at the Inter-Church Council of Greater New Bedford.

The Council consisted of a group of about 45 local Protestant churches with a building and central office on County Street in New Bedford. It was dedicated to helping the churches thrive and it ran several programs to benefit the community, especially the poor, the addicted and the defeated. The Council was funded by area churches and dedicated people in the community. One of the sponsor-saints, a doctor's wife, studied the stock market and grew the Council's investments to over $2,000,000. The Council also trained and supervised clergy who wanted to be certified as counselors. The ICC was a good place for me.

Chapter 19

The Inter-Church Council

I began as a volunteer with the ICC's Pastoral Care and Counseling Center. Those who came to our doors were often people who had no insurance and could not afford to pay private therapists. At the Center, clients paid what they could afford. The program also served those who sought a more spiritual orientation. After some months as a volunteer, I managed to prove that my skills were valuable and I was awarded the job of intake director at $14,000 a year. As such, I interviewed prospective clients and assigned appropriate counselors to each case.

Fortunately, we had a competent staff. At its height there were 14 counselors including four Catholic nuns. My role also included serving as the Protestant chaplain at St. Luke's Hospital in New Bedford, where I developed a team of volunteers to visit patients. One of my closest friends, Eric Lindell, Craig's father, was one. I had known him for years, beginning at Trinity Methodist in New Bedford where he served on the pastoral relations committee. He was a member of a team that came to Orleans to look me over, hear a sermon or two, and interview me for the job as pastor at Trinity. Eric would become an influential and enduring man in my life.

As chaplain, I attended the diagnostic meetings of the psychiatric staff which allowed me keep up on new developments in the field, especially in medications which were changing the lives of patients in new and promising ways.

At the ICC, I was privileged to work with local Protestant powerhouses including Sydney Adams, president of the Council. In his youth, he had been the lightweight boxing champion in England. He was popular for his wit and humor—and his vision. One group of women, "The Gay Ladies," prepared a 50-cent lunch when any Council group was meeting. They would do anything for Sydney.

The first time I met him was at a conference in Leominster, in Massachusetts, but a long way from home. At noontime, everyone left for the nearest restaurant and I stood there awkwardly, not knowing where to go. He looked my way and saw that I was at a loss so he asked me to have lunch with him. As we walked along, he kept up a patter.

"Have you ever had pizza?" he asked.

"No," I replied.

He was apparently into food and reflected on the life of a chef. "Most frustrated chefs work in restaurants with bars, but alcohol numbs the taste buds of drinkers, so they cannot fully appreciate the skill of the chef. They seldom get compliments."

"I hadn't thought about it," I replied. We found a decent-looking restaurant and sat down.

"Be right back," said Sydney as he hopped up and headed for the kitchen. He was gone about ten minutes and I wondered if I'd ever see him again. If I had tried such a thing, I would have been thrown out by my socks, but Sydney owned the world and thought nothing of invading the kitchen to meet the chef. Eventually the chef appeared with the most elaborate pizza I had ever seen. And to top it off, the pizza was on the house!

Sydney's special forte was working with the Council to create housing for low-income older folks. The successful high-rise, Melville Towers, in downtown New Bedford, a 320-unit housing complex for the elderly, built in 1975, was planned, financed and supervised by the Council. A smaller complex in the South End of New Bedford, Young House, provided elderly housing for 44 residents. Later, the beautiful Grinnell mansion on County Street was rehabilitated and offered 17 new units of housing for local seniors. So the ICC had a fine track record in housing as well as other areas.

My other great friend was David Goodenough, the director of psychological services at the Veterans Hospital in Brockton. He was a loyal volunteer and dedicated to the proposition that local pastors were key people in the delivery of mental health services. He attended every staff meeting for the 17 years I was there. Under his leadership the ICC became certified as a training center for pastoral counselors, a magnificent contribution to the ICC and the church community.

The Quality Circle

I wore many hats at the ICC, among them, program director of the Labor-Management Religion Collaborative, a job that took me into the business world to work as a counselor to factory workers. I was hired by Craig Lindell (Eric's son), the CEO at Fairhaven Corporation, to develop a program designed to increase quality and productivity in the manufacturing of women's handbags. American industry is based partly on an adversarial relationship between labor and management, and Craig wanted to foster more cooperation between the two.

One of the realities, for instance, is that employees know what works and what doesn't in the manufacturing process and very often they know how things might be done better. But they are not encouraged to speak up. Another reality is that these workers are responsible employees, even though they may suffer from depression, alcoholism and other problems. They deserve more than to be let go. This new program was an opportunity for them to get counseling on the job.

The plant manager, John Braga, had a swinging door concept about labor. If he didn't like someone, he could fire them—he had that kind of power. At the time Craig Lindell arrived at the helm, the company was suffering from a high turnover of employees, which was costly for the company. Even as a pastor at Trinity, I had heard about the company's lax hiring policy. If an alcoholic came in and asked for money, I would send him to Fairhaven Corporation to get a job. Craig felt that such constant hiring and firing cost the company more than if they provided the necessary support to people already working there.

When Craig took over, the company was not working up to its potential. Within five years, it was earning maybe ten million. The new engine of change was "the weekly meeting," or "quality circle" where employees could air their grievances and make suggestions. The term is borrowed from the Japanese but the process took an essentially American form here. The meetings included the plant manager, the workers, and John Braga, who was required to be there. If things weren't going well, this was everyone's chance to get it out. With this new focus on quality and productivity, the company was humming along and turning a nice profit. Then globalization intruded and changed the picture. China began flooding American markets with cheap handbags.

To stay in the game in the face of the Chinese, the company decided to upgrade their product from plastic to leather, which changed the whole procedure in the factory. And I learned a few things myself—how difficult it is to change anything, never mind everything. The workers' problems magnified in the face of change.

One particular afternoon was a disaster. The cutters had set the machines wrong and ruined $17,000 worth of leather. Our program went into action and the first thing we did was to establish a clear description of the product. The weekly "meeting" became ever more important.

A general work philosophy was developed. When workers walked in the door, they were to leave their credentials behind; everyone was equal and everyone was equally important in putting out the product. This was harder to follow than it seemed. For instance, one day two ladies had a complaint. They used glue in the operation and their big buckets got so thick with glue, they needed new ones. Other employees felt they were whining over nothing. The meeting failed when the two women left feeling angry, thinking they had not been heard. This set things back for a while. Something as small as replacing a dirty bucket, an item that ended up in the dump anyway, became a symbol of the difficulty of change.

Besides overseeing the new program, my role was to be a counselor to the workers. If an employee's productivity fell off, she might be given a warning but eventually she would see me, and I could help her get to the root of her problems. At the height of the program, I was seeing six employees a week. They were amazingly receptive to this on-the-job help.

On the whole, the workers loved the new ways. One day a forewoman came in and said that for years, she had longed to make suggestions but she feared she would be fired. Being able to speak up was such a great relief. In the new order, if a worker had a complaint, management had to come up with an answer before the next meeting a week later. The employees could finally say in the weekly meeting, "There you go again, John, you're not hearing us." It did wonders for morale. And I think John came to like it too.

All the workers did "piece work," meaning they were paid by their productivity per piece. One woman said there was something wrong with her machine and it was costing her too much energy and money to meet her quota. Bill, an industrial engineer who dealt with some of the mechanical problems, found that the piece had been put in upside down. The news went through the factory like wildfire; fixing the problem increased the woman's income considerably. In the past, she may not have complained, however burdened she was.

The employees also acted as testers and inspectors. If they felt a product had been poorly designed, they could shut down the factory and adjustments could be made. In this way, they were able to save the $17,000 they thought they had lost. Many workers in the city heard about the high morale at Fairhaven Corporation and quit their jobs elsewhere to work there, not because they would earn more but because they could have a voice and be an active part of the company.

Never underestimate the power of having a voice.

This fine story does not have a happy ending. The New York owners sold the factory. It closed within three years. A part of Craig Lindell's contract included ten percent ownership. I suspect he came out of it with several million dollars, which he used to develop businesses in Greater New Bedford, a city that desperately needs the work.

After 17 years with the Inter-Church Council, I retired when I was 75 because I was not functioning well. John Douhan, the director, asked me to resign and for good reason. I knew something was wrong. I had reached the point of being unable to add up a set of figures and I could not respond adequately to a telephone call. Two years later I was diagnosed with Parkinson's disease. I wasn't happy with the news but it gave me a reason why I was struggling so hard to be normal. More about Parkinson's later.

In 1985, the ICC got hit over the head when it took a loss of $300,000 on its group homes. The director had agreed to operate three group homes for the Department of Mental Retardation at the request of the state, which had promised to provide residents to the houses for 20 years if the Council would purchase them. So the Council agreed, given their fine record in housing for the elderly. But then Governor Weld came in and in a move to privatize state government, he turned over the operation of the program from the Department of Mental Retardation to the Center for Human Services in New Bedford. But the Center failed to pay its bills on time and the ICC was forced to evict their clients.

Dealing with the state is always risky and the Council took the loss. But the ICC is doing well today having gone through and recovered from the trauma. It is now active in a mentoring program for youngsters to keep them from dropping out of school; they continue their work in the hospital chaplaincy program and, of course, they maintain their excellent counseling service.

Chapter 20

My New Spiritual Home

After I left Trinity Methodist church to become a senior counselor at Rodman Job Corps, I was asked to conduct Sunday services at Smith Neck Friends Meeting in South Dartmouth. I felt connected to Quaker values and practices almost immediately, and this became my new spiritual home. In time, my family became members too.

The position came with a parsonage we didn't need since we had purchased our own home. It could not be rented since the member who had donated it stipulated that it must be the pastor's residence. We decided to make it a home for theological students who worked with the young people in our Quaker meeting, most of whom were enrolled in the divinity school in Boston. We got the word out and our first youth pastor was Howard Macy, an Old Testament scholar at Harvard. Howard did not plan to serve a parish for he had larger things in mind. His goal was to teach in a Quaker college. He was proficient in several languages and could easily get such a position. However, the unexpected happened. A warm relationship developed between Howard and the meeting; it took a bit longer for him to develop a relationship with the youth—the first year they "egged" the parsonage! Howard ended up staying seven years before becoming a professor at Fox University.

During the 1970s, a man named Gideon Howland and his wife Gertrude joined our prayer and study group. We would meet for an hour, spending the first half hour in quietness and the second half in sharing. Inspired by the sessions, the Howlands opened their little home to a meeting of young adults for coffee and conversations. It so happened that

Gideon and Gertrude had three beautiful daughters and male attendance climbed until there was no room for even one more seat. One night a young man even sat in the kitchen sink.

I was asked to join the group and give direction to the conversations and we ended up meeting for several years. Some of these people gathered in the afternoon to play a game called Michigan Rummy, a form of gambling. They played for pennies and tried hard to get me to join them. I would taunt them a little saying they'd be sorry if I ever got in their game. After all, I had the support of a higher up and could easily take their money. So one day I sat down and played two hands of cards. I took most of the money on the table and they never asked me to play again.

After that, I found an odorous chicken foot hanging from the rear view mirror of my car. I suspected Billy Reed was the culprit so I took the chicken foot home and put it in my freezer. At a Christmas party I made sure Billy Reed got the thing as a Christmas present. He opened it and turned red as a beet. I did not know how he dispensed with it. Two years later I officiated at his wedding and he presented me with a gift he asked me to open in front of all his guests so they could admire it. There was the chicken foot! And the place smelled to high heaven.

But in this case, a chicken foot is more than meets the eye. In my eyes, it became a symbol of the power of the small group and the bonding that goes on. I saw this transformation time and again. Small groups can move mountains. Several leaders came out of our own group. Charles Sisson attended for a time and he developed and directs Coastline Services for the Elderly, an organization that reaches across our entire region and helps older people in need.

Two valuable people at Smith Neck Friends Meeting are Billy and Deborah Reed (yes, that same Billy). Billy is a retired prison guard and now spends his time helping members of the meeting as well as his neighbors. Deborah is a registered nurse and works overtime due to the shortage of nurses.

When I look at my wife Christine's painting of a lone tree in our living room I think about the power of small groups. It's a large painting of a wind-shaped, stunted pine tree on a barren landscape. Long ago, we left Moorefield to drive an hour or so to reach a spot on top of the mountain called Dolly Sods. It was 30 degrees colder when we reached it and gale winds were blowing. Christine wanted to photograph the tree so she could paint it later. The finished painting is stark and striking, illustrating the impact of the empty space where century-old trees once stood. I think I would like it for the cover of this memoir. This single pine tree, unprotected by its kind, had no chance of growing tall and straight. It takes a community of trees to reinforce one another against the power of the wind. Standing alone it was twisted and deformed.

And so it is with people. There is power in small groups. The Quakers discovered the power of small groups by first noting that all great social changes begin in such groups, often with just a handful of people—the environmental movement, the women's movement. Truth emerges in the meeting of dedicated minds—in science, the arts, and in social action. The dynamics of the group brings out the value of the unique individual. The one absolute requirement of group dynamics is to be present, a real participant.

Religious authority, on the other hand, does not come from a group. It resides in the individual's relationship with God—there is no other necessary intervening force. Every Quaker is a minister. How simple and so true. The resources we require to solve our problems are right there in our relationships with others and with God, and nowhere else.

Disciplined silence is the most spiritual of all forms of worship, the foundation on which all meditations are based. It is rest for the weary soul. It is peace after conflict, based on the assumption that the search for trust and consensus cannot be achieved if one's communication is at fault. When we return to silence and listening, new insights will emerge.

Such concepts can be taught and many situations are open to the lesson. For instance, Christine and I were at the Rhode Island Watercolor Society to pick up her paintings when an angry lady came in to report that three young teens with skateboards were throwing rocks at the baby ducks on the pond. She spotted me, asked that I do something or call the police. I said I would talk to them.

I walked down the hill with her and asked her to wait. The boys, around 12, had leaned their boards against a tree and were taking turns jumping over a drainage ditch, keeping their eyes on my approach.

"How is the skateboarding?" I asked.

"They don't want us to skateboard in the park," said one with a rebellious look on his face.

"I want you to know you have a right to skateboard in the park, but the lady said you were throwing rocks at the baby ducks. You need to know that I own those baby ducks...and SO DO YOU. This is a public park and you have a say."

I returned to the boathouse to join Chris. When we were leaving the three boys were waiting for us.

"Do you really own the ducks?" they asked.

"Yes, I do. But remember I said you are part owners too."

"We want a skateboard park here. Can you get us a skateboard park paid for by the government?"

"No," I replied. "The President has gotten us in a war and there is no money from the government right now. But that is not the whole picture. I am a Quaker and the Quakers believe in the power of a small group. You are a small group. Three of you. If each one of you asked someone to join you, and they asked someone, you would be building a team. They may help just because you took action. A small group. Three of you!"

They were all smiles as they picked up their skateboards and left.

***

In the course of writing this memoir, I found a sermon I had delivered in January 1971 at Friends Meeting House in New Bedford. It is called:

"If I Had the Time"

James Truslow Adams, the American historian, wrote, "Perhaps it would be a good idea, fantastic as it sounds, to muffle every telephone, halt every motor, and stop all activity some day, to give people a chance to ponder for a few minutes on what it is all about, why they are living and what they really want."

Our social order will never stop to give us that moment, but we have the freedom to do so. The only problem is that our busyness defeats us: We say:

> If I had the time and place
> To sit me down full face to face
> With my better self which cannot show
> In my busy life which rushes so.
> I think I should find my soul
> Still climbing toward the shining Goal
> If I had the time and place.

Or:

Epitaph to a modern woman:

Here lies a poor woman…
Who was always busy
She lived at a pace that rendered her dizzy
She belonged to ten clubs, read Browning at sight
Was shown at luncheons and teas
And was out every night
She liked urges and splurges
Knew microbes by name
Approved of Del Sarto
Was daughter and dame
She golfed and Kodaked
And drove her own car
Her children she saw once in a while
Her husband wrote checks
And tried hard to smile
One day on her schedule she found an hour free
The shock was too great, she died instantly.

I wonder what her last words would have been like.

The custom of recording and remembering the last words of persons is not followed today as it was a generation or two ago. For one thing, most persons die quietly in their sleep in a hospital and do not pronounce any last words consciously. Too often we do not know we are dying. But it is an interesting matter to recall some last words that have been recorded. Many of them show great courage and unshaken faith, unafraid of any amazement.

One notable last remark may not seem to display any pious mood, yet it is a word of high faith. This is the last sentence, said by my professor, Samuel F. Upham, a man of great learning, wit, and faith, and for many years a teacher at Drew Theological Seminary. His family reported: When the end was near, family and friends gathered at his bedside. Someone said Dr. Upham was already dead. Another said, "Feel his feet. No one ever died with warm feet." Then Dr. Upham opened an eye and said, "Joan of Arc did." Those were his last words. And they were great ones. For the wit and humor persisting to the very end were the expressions of a high faith without fear.

Some of the last words that are well known were those of John Wesley. He said, "The best of all is, God is with us."

Oliver Cromwell is reported as saying to those around him, "Will no one here thank God?"

In our own day there is that beautiful last sentence said by Dr. Peter Marshall to his wife as the men from an ambulance carried him out after his heart attack, "I'll see you in the morning." This is what death means to a Christian.

Our last words are often expressive of the life we live. Some are neither noble nor words of faith.

Think of the last words of P.T. Barnum, the circus man who said during his life, "A sucker is born every moment." His last words were "What were today's receipts?"

Or Henry Hazlitt, the 19th century essayist, who said, "Well, I've had a happy life." That showed a large spirit, with no bitter complaint, but think more deeply. It is not enough to have had a happy life. Parasites can be happy.

Contrast all this with the words of Jesus on the cross, "It is finished." He had been given a work to do and he had accomplished it. The acceptance of a great commission from God lifts life out of triviality and selfishness.

The greatest of last words are those of Jesus, "Father, into thy hands I commit my spirit." Jesus said this at the end of his life, but he also said it at the beginning of his ministry at the temptation. They are words to say at the beginning and all the way through to the end.

How do we initially give and then maintain that kind of commitment?

It comes through a life of prayer.

***

Chapter 21

A Long Friendship

My friendship with Fay Gemmell, my old classmate from Boston University School of Theology, has endured and grown stronger over the years. We have talked our way through life, supporting each other, listening to each other, asking advice, sharing doubts, hopes and dreams and, of course, having fun. Our families meshed immediately, emotionally and psychologically.

Both Fay and I were from farm communities and had little interest in sports. Fay majored in psychology at Boston University under Dr. Paul Johnson, while I majored in sociology with Dr. Walter Mulder, who specialized in social ethics. We were both drawn to pastoral counseling. Eventually Fay was awarded his doctorate, which I never finished, as I was unable to prove my thesis about religious values in mixed marriages. We both served five small Methodist churches over a period of 20 years, then left the ministry for pastoral counseling. I became a counselor at the Job Corps and at mental health centers and he became a pastoral counselor at Keene College in New Hampshire.

On a masculine-feminine scale, people might say we were on the feminine side, but not homosexual. We were happily married and had families. As ministers, we wished to help people and work to correct some of the world's injustices. We believed in the equality of people and wanted to confront racism and other evils.

In those days, one's sexual orientation was the most hidden of all subjects, especially being gay. The Broadway play, "Tea and Sympathy" was groundbreaking in its time and attempted to deal with the problem. In one of the funniest scenes the leading character's friend tries to teach him to walk differently. A musician, he was on the effeminate side of the scale, uninterested in contact sports and displaying a keen sensitivity to others. His roommate talked him into visiting a prostitute, which turned him off. The football coach's wife offered him tea and sympathy and attempted to seduce him to prove to him that he was not gay. In the end, it is the coach who turns out to be gay.

Fay and I spent a lot of time discussing the best way to raise our children. We decided to handle matters of the human body in a completely natural, honest way, treating it not as an object of shame but of respect and sex as a normal, natural activity. We took great pains not to have our children feel shame.

Thanksgiving was always a special time for our families—we had Thanksgiving together for close to three decades. Eventually we began including foreign students such as Ayrton Pinto from Brazil, a young violinist. His parents did not approve of his girlfriend and so they sent him off to be educated. The poor man needed a family and we became it. Eventually he became a member of the Boston Symphony. Another was Mona Sing from India who always brought Indian dishes she'd prepared. Our Thanksgiving dinners with the Gemmells went on for 29 years until our children were all married and setting up Thanksgiving dinners of their own.

Fay and his wife Charlotte were opposites in temperament. Charlotte thrived amid the disorder caused by five young children and handled the household remarkably well given that she did not even have a washing machine until after the birth of their third child. Once when we were visiting, a child appeared and asked for clean underwear. Charlotte went to a closet, opened the door and a flood of clean clothes spilled out. She found what was needed, piled the clothes back in, closed the door and did not miss a beat in the conversation. Later, in her teaching career in New Hampshire, she was cited as the teacher of the year by the state. A good mother, a great teacher.

Fay, on the other hand, had a need for order and he created it by retreating to his study. That room was a masterpiece of order and one could not help noticing artistic excellence in its décor.

During the Vietnam years, when liberals were treated as pariahs (before the tide turned), a rumor was flying about that Fay was having a relationship with a male student at Keene College where he was campus minister. I got wind of the rumor and called him. Fay replied that this was the tip of the iceberg. The same was being said of a liberal professor and priest. Because Fay expressed liberal views in his preaching and weekly newspaper column, certain people were out to get him.

We agreed to meet at Dr. David Landau's clinic for a conference. Dr. Landau was a friend that Fay and I had been working with for several years in the field of alcoholism treatment. Over time, we nurtured his friendship and looked to him for help with ministerial and career problems. He owned a 30-bed hospital where he allowed us to stay when we came to Boston for conferences and professional gigs. I felt fortunate that I had become a part of a team that Dr. Landau recognized as competent therapists, thanks to our training in counseling at BU.

Fay was indeed under attack because of his general liberalism and outspoken views on the Vietnam War. He even received threatening calls in the middle of the night, warning him that his daughter might get hit by a car as she walked to school. The caller suggested he go back to Russia where he belonged. Dr. Landau believed Fay must confront his attackers and so Fay began working with the Keene chief of police who planted a reporter in the local chapter of the John Birch Society. This worked. They nabbed the people making the threats and the harassment stopped.

In fact, Fay was not a very scary man. He was friendly to all and went out of his way to help anyone in need.

One day he saw an elderly lady slowly walking up Beacon Street, a cane and a bundle in each hand. Dressed in long black clothes, beads hanging to her waist, she seemed to need an assist.

"May I help you?" he asked.

"Young man, where are your wings?" she asked, astonished.

She was Mrs. Percival Lowell, 90, wife of the astronomer whose mathematical skills pointed to where the planet Pluto ought to be. Fay relieved her of the bundles so she was free to manage the canes. They became friends because she trusted him.

On the 25th anniversary of Fay's column in the Keene Sentinel, he was celebrated by the editor: "A quarter of a century in the land of Yankee Puritanism hasn't erased the lessons of the Nebraska prairies. He traces his life-long interest in people and causes to the loneliness of those prairies and his ecumenical outlook to that Bible Belt...He searches for answers in the daily comings and goings of his friends and neighbors, in the ups and downs of family life and the latest headline."

Chapter 22

Jane Merchant, Mentor and Poet

I don't remember when I first read a poem by Jane Merchant. I do remember it was filler in a national magazine, and I think I came across it during my West Roxbury pastorate when the difficulty of that ministry was getting me down and leaving me weary. I almost missed it. All it said was:

> My feet feel mired
> My head feels hazy
> I hope I'm tired
> I'm afraid I'm lazy

Well, it must have captured my mood at that very moment and I have been singing her praises ever since. I went out and bought her first volume of daily devotional readings, and by the time I was pastor of Trinity Methodist in New Bedford, I was including a Jane Merchant poem in most sermons, funerals and weddings. I have given away hundreds of copies to parishioners and friends. Altogether she published 11 books of humor and religious poetry. Her most popular was a book of devotions in poetry and prayer based on 1 Corinthians 1:13. One poem reads:

> If I Have Not Love

> Men send their speech across blue miles of space,
> Across great continents their words ring clear,
> Yet all their eloquence does not efface

The mountain barriers of hate and fear.
Men chaff the heavens' mysteries, have explained
The atom, given their bodies to be burned
In war's fierce hells; and yet have never gained
The good for which their hearts have always yearned.

And I—ah, well indeed, dear Lord, I know
That all I can say, or think, or do
Is utter nothingness, an idle show,
If I have not deep love, sincere and true;
Love for thy loveliness in star and tree,
Love for my fellow men, pure love for thee.

I think of Jane Merchant as "the sensitizer." That is the effect her poetry and prayers had on me. I watched that reaction in others and it is one of the reasons I gave away so many of her books. She had an extraordinary influence on one of my parishioners at Trinity, in particular. His name was Harold Babcock and he had an anxious mother, a trait she passed on to her son. When I was making my rounds in the hospital, I discovered he was a patient. He was so upset at the possibility that something might be wrong with him, he seemed to be climbing the walls. And something was wrong. The next morning he had a section of intestine removed and it was malignant, which made him even more anxious. Harold was a traveling salesman and had a trip scheduled to Knoxville, Tennessee. I suggested that he stop in and see Jane Merchant. He did and his outlook began to change. Trust took the place of his anxiety and negative feelings. If there was going to be pain in his future he could handle it.

Who was Jane Merchant? And where did she get the power of personality that led to the impact she had on others through her writing? Jane has a fascinating biography. She was born with brittle bone disease and, as a result, her bones never hardened. When she was four years old, her father attempted to pick her up and broke both her legs and arms. She was never able to walk. And she was stone deaf by the time she was 20, so fragile that she could be fractured by being turned over in bed. Her family were subsistence farmers and devoted to her care. Her father rented farmland and at one point in her life had dairy cows. Her sister became a nurse and for years she administered hot compresses to keep Jane from going blind.

Jane was shy and admitted others into the reality of her life only with great anxiety. Writing was her salvation. She loved to write, which she could really do. She would write short four line poems and one day she mustered the courage to send them to national magazines. The first one was accepted and paid her one dollar. Thus began her career as a most sensitive and creative interpreter of the religious life of the nation.

I was privileged to correspond with her and contribute to her biography.

> You think me deaf? I heard a snowflake fall.
> I heard a rainbow singing; and the faint,
> Blue shadowed melody that twilight plays
> On spinet trees; and I heard the quaint
> Elf music made by moon-beams on still waters,
> And heaven's anthems as the stars appear;
> And once I heard a star…Oh, I have music
> Sweeter than sounds that reach the outer ear!

Jane Merchant's biography, written by Sarah J. Ricketts, says, "All along, the conviction has grown that Jane somehow knew how it feels to be me, to be human. I wanted to discover Jane and found that in the process, she helped me discover more of myself." The biography opens with this poem:

> In a certain sullen wall
> That shuts the spacious world from view
> Chance—or miracle—has made
> A space for looking through;
>
> A little blessed window space
> Through which imprisoned eyes may see
> An upward-going leafy road,
> A tiny flowering tree;
>
> And, growing close and pressing inward
> Through the window in the wall,
> Sprays of blossom shaped to music,
> White and sweet and small.
>
> In whatever walls surround us,
> Stubborn walls of grief or pain

175

Barred by gates that will not open
While our lives remain,

God's love is a window, showing
Us a wide and leafy land,
And his mercy, bell-like, blossoms,
Sweetly, close at hand.

Her reaction to social evil is best seen in her poem, "Outlander":

"I thought someone was knocking." She stood eager
As anyone can be who's almost lost
The use of hope, holding the warped door open—
The door with its clean threshold still uncrossed,
After long months, by any foot but hers—
Speaking to silence, as the lonely will
Who listen for replies that never come.
She saw the houses tumbling down the hill
And women talking in the yard nearby.
She stared at them. One turned away her head,
And then they turned around and went inside.
"It must have been the wind. Of course," she said.
"It must have been." And then she flung the door
Wide open, bowing to the icy blast
That rushed into the room. "Come right on in,"
She said to it. "I'm glad you have come at last.
Now sit right down and make yourself at home.
This chair's the best one. Let me fix a cup
Of something hot to warm you. It's cold out.
Yes, it's too cold now, but it may warm up.
It may warm up someday." She wasn't crying.
It was too late. She just sat talking there
And talking to the wind. Cold as it was,
It was her warmest neighbor anywhere.

Another great influence on me is Abraham Lincoln. Years ago my family gave me the six-volume set of the "Life of Lincoln" by Carl Sandburg. I have read it six times over my lifetime. The writing has had a profound influence on me.

Chapter 23

Thoughts on This and That

In my lifetime, the religious right has grown immensely and become a powerful religious and political force. Their religion emphasizes Jesus but, in fact, the leaders rely mostly on Old Testament codes of conduct and ignore the teachings of Jesus as applied to everyday life. Jesus said—"You have been taught of old 'an eye for an eye and a tooth for a tooth' but I have you a new commandment: Love one another, respect one another. You are the children of God."

If you want to know what God is like, consider the father in the parable of the Prodigal Son. God's nature and ethics are revealed in it. If you want to understand his expectations of us in our behavior as servants in his kingdom, study the parable of the Good Samaritan.

The religious right relies on a view of the Bible as reliable and true in all its parts, but you surrender your intellect if you believe this. The Bible is a record of man's search for meaning in life. It is history, not a guide for judgment. A guide for judgment requires no facing of doubts, no sense of meaning. It casts decision-making in black and white terms, but rarely are things black and white. It does not allow for the gray areas. I have noticed a common refrain in material sent out by religious right leaders: Every sermon preached, every newsletter written portrays God as angry, vengeful, punishing and mean. Man is always wrong and in need of punishment. I do not believe this.

I agree with the Quakers who believe there is that of God in every human being. Therefore every person is sacred. You cannot consciously harm another human being. Religious authority resides in the individual's relationship with God, and there is no other necessary intervening force. And did I say—Every Quaker is a minister?

More Quakerisms—Disciplined silence is the most spiritual of all forms of worship, the foundation on which all meditations are based and rest for the weary soul. When we return to silence and listening, new insights will emerge. But one must be present, engaged. And how do Quakers bring about change? We emphasize "persuasion." Persuasion is mightier than war. Mightier than bombing people into oblivion.

That "Born Again" bumper sticker so dear to the religious right implies that God made some mistakes as he created us and we have to be born again. I say man was made right the first time, but we have not lived up to our potential. Our task is to build community. We have no other choice. The dean at Boston University Chapel said it right in dedicating a Chair: "Mr. Daniels has learned there is no place to hide in this world except in the hearts of our fellow man." This concept urges us to have respect for all persons. Respect is a huge word. My father taught me to respect others, for this confirms the value and humanity of the person. Respect the truth. Your word is your bond.

Respect became a much-used word during the Johnson administration with LBJ's creation of "The Great Society." Federal money began flowing into the inner cities and organizers and social workers had to learn to respect disadvantaged people of all races and ethnic groups and work with them, or nothing could be accomplished.

I am constantly amazed and saddened by the way gambling has become such an accepted part of our society. This past week I stopped for gas and watched a young lady, not yet 20, purchase $20 worth of lottery tickets. Just one of the many temptations faced by the young, never mind the old. I wanted to ask her how much she had spent and what she had won since playing the game. If only I could have shared some lessons I had learned from my parents and the Methodist church: gambling is always a losing proposition. There is a better way—put your money in the bank and let it draw compound interest.

When I was counseling at the Inter-Church Council, I had a client who would steal his wife's paychecks to buy tickets. He couldn't stop because he kept trying to get back all the money he had lost. He lived in a state of hidden rage. Those who think casinos will save our cities ought to spend some time at a counseling center. Gambling destroys individuals, it destroys families. The return is very little when you add it up.

My life has encompassed several revolutions: Blacks, Women, Sex, Technology. Back in graduate school, I took Dr. John Green's course at BU on Marriage and the Family. In one assignment, I was sent to the cemetery at the Old South Church in Boston and told to collect the birth and death dates of each woman buried there. The average age of death was 39.

Dr. Green gave a description of what life was like for Victorian women. Married at puberty, a woman had little say about whom she would marry. She could not refuse her husband's sexual demands and hence was pregnant every year. She could not own property, or vote, or hold most jobs except those of maid or housekeeper. When she gave birth she was on her own. If she had a doctor, he probably tended to his horse before tending to her and didn't wash. It was commonplace for women to die in childbirth, as my little trip to the cemetery showed.

And look where women are today. In this country, their progress has been astonishing. Their voices are heard everywhere in our society. In much of the world, however, they have not made much progress. In fact, they are still in the Stone Age, the property of men.

As for the sexual revolution, it's moving along at a fast clip. No one need push it along. It's racing all by itself.

And life in this country changed for blacks with the Civil Rights Act, led by President Lyndon Johnson in the 1960s. Goodbye segregation. And now we are looking at our first Black president of the United States. Though I will not see a woman become president in my lifetime, I feel optimistic about the future of blacks and women in the U.S. I believe I contributed to that progress by being in the Workshop for Equality, by being a mentor and counselor to poor black boys, and by preaching love and equality. And now we have to keep going.

We don't teach the young that paying taxes is a patriotic act. All you ever hear is griping about having to pay. But taxes support the common good, our schools, our libraries, our parks. The most fair tax is the graduated income tax based on the ability to pay.

I never did like titles. I have always felt that the universal title of Mr., Mrs., and Ms. was enough for anybody. An Episcopal rector in New Bedford always insisted on being called "Father." I was castigated for failing to call a particular preacher "doctor." His doctorate was from a mail order company. Remember—Mr., Mrs. and Ms. covers everybody.

I remember the refrain from an old song:

You cannot make a gooseberry pie out of a goose
Don't try it, it cannot be done
You cannot get milk from a gentleman cow
Don't try it, it cannot be done
You cannot successfully counsel members of your own family
Don't try it, it cannot….

I tried it when my brother Rodney and his wife Marilyn were at odds. She had a violent temper and broke all the dishes in the house. I tried it again when my son Jim and his first wife separated. It cannot be done; my emotions were too involved. Counseling takes maturity and listening skills and these skills develop over time. It also takes objectivity. My three sons are all in second marriages. They now know how to communicate, how to love and especially how to forgive.

One of the greatest influences on my life has certainly been music, and I think perhaps I have not appreciated the impact of the Seminary Singers tour on my religious thought and feelings. The words of the 130th Psalm set to music by the director Dr. James Houghten closed each of the thirty-five concerts we sang on that trip. My friend Fay Gemmell was trying to highlight its impact when he wrote—

"In the beginning was the music and the music was in the heart of God. And as he created, he sang and his creation sang back."

The 130th Psalm expresses my deepest religious feelings:

Out of the deep have I called unto Thee, O Lord,
Lord, Hear my voice.
O let Thine ears be attentive to the voice of my supplications.
If, thou Lord, shouldst mark my iniquities
Oh, Lord, who could abide it.
For there is mercy with thee, that thou may be feared.
I looked for the Lord. My soul waits for him
and in his word do I trust.
My soul waits for the Lord more than the morning watch,
more than the watch.
Oh, Israel, hope in the Lord, for with the Lord there is plenteous redemption,
and he will redeem Israel from all his sin.

Chapter 24

Returning to Moorefield

Every summer and Christmas, the Bean family returned to Moorefield to visit my family and Chris's parents and old friends and neighbors. Over the years, our sons bonded with that mountain landscape and farm-studded valley, remote enough to keep its quirks and misty timelessness. So in a sense we always returned to the same place where not much was changed. And yet everything had changed.

Take the pine tree. When I worked that summer at Lost River State Park, we were aware of a landscape dominated by a lone pine tree, a sight that always took our breath away. So alone and so powerful in its aloneness, the pine tree defined the area and, in fact, ruled over it. You could so clearly see it from a distance as you left Baker's Post office at the junction of Baker Creek and Lost River. Today the new highway, characterized by "long stretches of steel and concrete" eight lanes wide, spans from ridge to ridge, covering the area like a blanket so you can scarcely see the pine tree, now far below the height of the span. The pine tree gorge, as I call it now, is just another spot on the map.

At the old homestead, however, everything was the same, except Mother and Dad kept growing older, as Chris and I do today. Mother still baked her good biscuits and Dad, who had happily retired from his various businesses, kept busy with the farm.

My other reason for going home, of course, was to fish a stretch of the "Big River," the south fork of the Potomac that traversed the valley up river to Petersburg. And I could still find fishing companions by sniffing around the neighborhood. They were easy to round up here, unlike in the

181

Northeast where everyone is so busy all the time. One such fisherman was my old neighbor, Mr. Coward. He and his wife once owned and operated the Heritage Inn in Petersburg and they dutifully promoted local artists like Ellen Elms whose landscapes always brought us home. We own two of her beautiful watercolors.

Anyway, I was up river with Mr. Coward when he called over for me to give him a hand. I could see his arm was entangled in fishing line.

"Quick, get the hook out." It was well embedded in his arm and no way could I pull it out.

"This is a task for Doc Maxwell."

Doc had been the valley doctor for about 24 years and was trying hard to retire and get a young doctor to take his place. Without Dr. Maxwell, the nurse practitioner would have had to cover the entire valley. We found Doc splitting and stacking wood for the winter. When he saw how deep the hook had penetrated, he said he would need a pair of pliers to cut the hook and push the point through the skin. Since he could not find his surgical pair, he was forced to use ordinary pliers and was definitely having trouble.

"What a tough old codger you are," Doc kept saying as he worked.

"Well, I guess that ends the fishing for the day," I said once the hook was removed and I could see his arm bleeding under the band-aids.

"Not for me," said Mr. Coward, so we headed back to the river. Now that is a very good reason to return to Moorefield. It was no accident that the followers of Jesus were fishermen! So it shall ever be.

We also retained our good friendship with the Weese family. Earl, a master carpenter, had access to the rare lumber being shipped in from tropical forests. His china closets were masterpieces. His sister Kathleen had married Earnest Puffenberger who owned the local jewelry store. They were great game players, contagious games that Chris and I picked up and play to this day.

When my father died at 79, he was a respected businessman known for being genuine, a man of integrity. His illness was sudden. In fact, we were on our way to West Virginia for a visit. When I called Mother, she said Father had a terrible headache and the doctor recommended he be taken to the hospital in Winchester 75 miles away. When we arrived, we were told he had an attack of shingles in the brain and was extremely ill. We drove on home that night so Mother could get some sleep. The next day we returned to Winchester prepared to stay indefinitely. The family doctor told us he was brain dead and that if he survived he would live in a vegetative state. He had maybe five days to live unless we hooked him up to artificial supports. But Father had expressed the wish that he die naturally so we agreed there would be no life supports and went back to Moorefield.

Meanwhile, our family doctor went on vacation. The backup doctor was Catholic and immediately hooked my father up to all the new equipment the hospital was experimenting with. He said, as long as there was life, there was hope and he was in charge. Father lived another month under these awful conditions leaving Mother with thousands of dollars in unnecessary bills. He would have hated that!

He believed he had left her enough income, $400 a month to see her through. Little did he know she would be a widow for 23 years. Ten years before he died, he left me title to the farm, noting that my brother was not as good a manager. It caused some ruffled feathers, as you might imagine. The farm (he called it a ranch) was Father's retreat. He cleared brush, planted trees, especially pines and walnuts and attempted to grow ginseng. Since no one actually lived there, the ground moles had their way. I rented the farm out after his death, which supplemented Mother's income. Rodney would help out occasionally but he lived in Washington and that's where he stayed.

Mother soldiered on. She developed breast cancer when she was 80 and had one breast removed. A few years later, she had the other removed. When she was dying, Kathleen was the one I turned to. Mother was 97 that sad spring when I made three trips back to Moorefield. Fortunately, I was there when she died. Kathleen gave me the name of Mrs. Maxine Cullers who lived up the South Fork beyond the Trumbo Gap. Mrs. Cullers had gone with Kathleen when Mother developed pneumonia and had to be taken to the hospital 75 miles away.

She and her family lived in a beautiful wilderness in a house her son had built across the river. The only access was a swinging bridge. Every piece of lumber, every utility was carried across that swinging bridge. In better days, I had experienced some of the best small mouth bass fishing I had ever known as the only access is through the land owned by the Cullers.

Mother lived a good life and was much loved by her family and neighbors. I have only happy memories of this frontier woman who so believed in culture in a place that, well, was not very cultured. Long ago she fell in love with her teacher and that was a very good day. The rest is family history.

Chapter 25

Living With Parkinson's

When I reached my 75th birthday, I was having nightmares and trouble swallowing. My responses were slow. Chris was worried and tried to account for my loss of laughter, the mask-like features on my face and my terrible fatigue. One evening I tried to add up a column of figures and could not.

I went to see Dr. Bruce Abbott, a local neurologist, and he said my symptoms indicated I had Parkinson's disease. He gently said the disease would lead to a progressive deterioration of bodily function by my failure to produce carbidopa. It would not kill me right away but, sure as hell, would mess up my life. Dr. Abbott said there was massive research going on but no one knows what causes it. Pesticides are suspected. He prescribed Sinemet and said I had a life expectancy of ten years.

Dr. Edward Hirlihy, my primary physician, placed me on B-12 injections once a month for the rest of my life. I had other symptoms that were developing fast and all required medicine. Then I had two minor strokes.

Marcia Glynn, a nurse and fellow Quaker, persuaded me to consult with a professional in the study of Parkinson's at Beth Israel in Boston. She also has Parkinson's and so we have traveled together for appointments with Dr. Edmond Pasquale Leone ever since.

Not long after I faced this grim reality, I attended an art show in Tiverton, RI when a woman touched me on the shoulder and said, "You have Parkinson's, don't you?"

"How do you know?" I asked.

"I watched you walk across the grass. Your gait told me."

The costs of medications became astronomical. In 1986 tax returns, I reported $10,400 for prescription drugs. This did not include the drugs Chris takes.

The nearest active support group was in Middleboro and Chris and I attended meetings there led by tall, handsome Tom Pinkerton. Helen Morrison, another active member, brought her mother who was in a wheelchair. The speakers spoke on many aspects of Parkinson's and the group was a wonderful support but when Tom left the community, it folded. Members of the group helped me start a similar group in Dartmouth and we meet at the Dartmouth senior center. We now have 35 members.

My later years have been active, contemplative and really quite fine, except for the Parkinson's. The Methodist church unexpectedly came through for my retirement. After serving in five Methodist churches way back when, I left the ministry and withdrew my pension, thinking I could invest the money for more return. I had forgotten the church's policy to match my contributions. When I turned 70 or so, I received a notice from the board asking me how I would like to receive my pension. I had no idea there was anything there! The church's contribution of $4000 had grown to nearly $80,000. Now, that was kind of a nice surprise for this old retiree.

One of the hardest things about growing old is losing old friends. I had to say goodbye to my soul brother, Eric Lindell, this year, 2008, and that was one of my saddest moments. I was supposed to give the eulogy, but my Parkinson's made such a mess of me that day, I couldn't even make it to the service. It was very stressful for me not to be there.

I continue my friendship with Eric's son, Craig, who has an inspiring story of his own. He failed in school because of a learning disability, mixing up letters and numbers and seemingly not making progress. His problem was dyslexia but at the time this condition had not been identified. No one understood how gifted a child he was! His father had given up on him and encouraged him to train for a trade. Nonetheless Craig was accepted at Bates with very little chance of succeeding and guess what? His brilliance was discovered and nurtured, and he graduated from Bates tenth in his class.

Craig went on to become a future-minded entrepreneur, quite different from your ordinary businessman. He seems to listen to the universe and hear what is being asked of him. I know this sounds odd, but I believe it is true. As I related previously, he ran Fairhaven Corporation after his father retired from that position, and operated it based on the Japanese model of quality circles, a very brave thing to do in this gritty manufacturing city. His wife Melanie is a fine teacher and she helped my son John learn the computer when he worked there for a summer. He later turned his skills into a career. Craig's brother Carl was a super-salesman for the company, and knew his customers so well, his buyers actually asked him to make the buying decisions. So we have a special family here, not just smart but caring, and sometimes it felt as if we were one big family.

When the New York Co. sold the business, he used the money to invent, create and reach for clean solutions to nagging, dirty problems. Passionately interested in the environment, today he invents green ways of doing things and is having great success. Just now he is involved in turning wastewater into potable water.

We live in a watery place and Craig and I have spent many a leisure hour exploring its waterways and inlets, waterfowl and wildlife. Beautiful Dartmouth has always been on the verge of overdevelopment and we a have tried to help the town keep her wild places and sanctuaries. We were not always successful against forces so much bigger than we were.

Citizens can see a town changing from many different perspectives and Craig and I kept an eye on Dartmouth from the water. We liked to take the canoe around Padanaram Harbor and down the Paskamansett River to see the great horned owls that nested in the tall trees. Since the building of the North Dartmouth Mall, fallen trees and thick underbrush have become part of the landscape and we wanted to see how the owls were doing. Thank goodness, the owls' location in the flood plain had saved them. We first made this trip when public argument was at its loudest about where the mall would be built. It turned out that the public did not have much to say about things.

The Paskamansett River had been one of four unpolluted rivers on the east coast and the mall came to overshadow it. Among other things, we were worried about the runoff from hundreds of cars in the parking lot where their dripping oil would eventually get into the river unless there were built-in holding tanks to catch the oil. We lost on that issue too. Now, on our trips, we can find patches of oil in the sand. So there are now three unpolluted rivers on the east coast. And this would be only the first of many malls in Dartmouth.

On this particular day I put my casting rod in the canoe and forgot about the world. As we toured the harbor, the water was calm. I made several casts while we were on the way under the bridge as we decided to go to the outer harbor. A large blue fish struck at the lure, missed and hit the top of the canoe. It looked about ten pounds—a blue fish this size could take a good bite out of you. We decided to keep fishing and canoeing separate after this. But fish still played a large role in my life, until Parkinson's.

But my fishing days have not gone away. I see them in my dreams.

In the winter of 1990, Chris had a benign growth removed from her liver. It was a frightening time for us, and we decided to look again at our priorities after this close call. Chris had yearned for a studio addition to the house so she could do her painting, and our savings and investments had produced enough money for us to do it. A dream come true. She had been relegated to the basement for so long and the lighting was not great for this Monet.

A local builder planned the studio to rest on the driveway and we watched this magnificent project grow from day to day. Also, it brought some unexpected excitement to the Bean household. A crawl space of about 18 inches was left open on the south side. The west end had a basement window which offered a clear view into the crawl way.

During the great 2003 snowstorm, a feral cat spent the night in a leaf-filled window well and slowly made its way in the deep snow to the south opening. It had difficulty getting under the top of the opening because of a huge pile of hair on its back. We believed it was injured and I called the animal control officer. For four days the animal ignored the food and trap. We could see some movement occasionally when we looked in from the covered basement. By the fifth day, both the officer and I assumed it was dead. She pushed an extension pole in and pulled out the body of a very large opossum.

"It's dead all right," she said, as she plopped it in a plastic bag. "Under the law, if it's alive and uninjured, I would have to release it where I found it. Congratulations on not having a skunk in there. You might have had to move out for a year."

Yes, our luck. Of the feral cat? No sign. The next day our neighbor confirmed that her daughter had been feeding the cat for a year. He was badly wounded and would not have survived the storm. They offered me the lumber to seal in the south side opening, which I thought was a good idea. Whenever I have a project involving lumber and tools, I call on my musical son Jim. He arrived ready to go, took one look and said—"cinder blocks" and he ordered up seven for eight dollars and nary a critter can get in there now. Of course, that's when I began to worry that we may have trapped other animals who could not get out.

But the point of all this is that Chris got her dream studio, skylight and all, and even into her 80s, she is in there painting everyday, doing beautiful landscape work and making a big name for herself. Her art is exhibited in public places all around town. She is amazingly disciplined; the little girl who loved art and refused to give it up when she became a minister's wife. She has a gift but having a gift is not enough. You have to do the work to nurture and cultivate that gift. This she has done; she has pursued excellence. Art is the guiding spirit of her life.

Our three sons each have one child, and we are happy grandparents. Devin was born on March 15, 1989 to Charles and Eileen Bean. For all his rebellious years, Charles ended up with a distinguished career as a librarian at the Library of Congress in Washington, DC. There is something to be said for taking a troubled kid out of a troubled environment. Whisking him off to private school in New Hampshire was exactly the thing to do. Eileen is a retired attorney for the commerce department.

Nathan was born on December 23, 1987 to James and Cindy. James teaches music at Friends Academy in Dartmouth and Cindy is a New Bedford social worker. Jim is well known in the area for his superb musicianship.

Jessamyn Lindstrom Bean was born on October 10, 1982. She is the daughter of John and Rebecca Bean who are divorced. John lives in Attleboro, MA with his girlfriend Stephanie Weiz and her daughter Sarah McClanahan. We worried about John because he always fled conflict in the family and we rather wished he'd stay around and fight it out. When arguments broke out, John retreated to his room. He hated the ongoing conflict between Charles and Jim. But John survived our family and today he is a whiz at a computer company.

An interesting threesome, our sons—a librarian, a musician and a computer geek. That's what our sons have become and, more important, they are wonderful human beings.

Burial Instructions

My Parkinson's disease has spurred me to take action and make my final wishes known. I wrote to the Quaker Monthly Meeting and requested that my ashes be scattered in the woods surrounding the old Apponagansett Meeting House in Dartmouth. This imposing wooden structure on a rugged hill is one of the first Quaker sites in the area and in its side yard is an old burial ground, a lovely old place where the living find solace and the dead live on, at least in spirit. It is truly the place for me because for the last 20 years I have kept the woods free of dead trees and trimmed the white pines as they grew taller. Just outside of the rock wall, a holly tree took root and I have watched it grow. It is about seven feet tall as I write.

I requested that my ashes be spread on the forest floor on the north end of the cemetery where the holly tree is growing. I want my ashes to feed the tree—that would make me happy. If a plaque is needed to comfort visitors at this, my final resting place, let it be small and biodegradable.

***

Breinigsville, PA USA
30 December 2009
229937BV00001B/73/P